Backyard Ducks and Geese

A Practical Guide for the
Enthusiast and the Smallholder

Backyard Ducks and Geese

A Practical Guide for the Enthusiast and the Smallholder

J. C. Jeremy Hobson

Photographs by Rupert Stephenson

THE CROWOOD PRESS

First published in 2009 by
The Crowood Press Ltd
Ramsbury, Marlborough
Wiltshire SN8 2HR

www.crowood.com

British Library Cataloguing-in-Publication Data
A catalogue record for this book is available from the British Library.

ISBN 978 1 84797 132 6

Illustration Acknowledgements
All the photographs in this book are courtesy of Rupert Stephenson,
poultry photographer (www.rupert-fish.co.uk).

Line illustrations by Keith Field.

Disclaimer
The author and the publisher do not accept any responsibility in any
manner whatsoever for any error or omission, nor any loss, damage,
injury or liability of any kind incurred as a result of the use of any of the
information contained in this book, or reliance upon it.

Typeset by Carreg Limited, Ross-on-Wye, Herefordshire

Printed and bound in India by Replika Press

Contents

Dedication

To my mother, who always insisted that I should use my full Christian names on book titles. Without such advice, I could easily have been confused on the Internet with an eminent American preacher and writer!

Acknowledgements

Of course, first and foremost I must thank Rupert Stephenson; as yet I have never had the good fortune to meet him personally, but I have had much correspondence with him over several years. His photos have illustrated not only several of my books, but also many of my articles in *Smallholder* magazine. Rupert Stephenson is a groundsman and a true countryman, with an excellent eye for poultry; he is, without question, one of the best known poultry photographers in the UK today. Having first studied digital photography at Hereward College, his work has since been reproduced in all the leading poultry magazines; it appears on many web sites, and is used frequently by the Smithsonian Institute in America. Born in Coventry in 1959, he has kept bantams all his life; he decided many years ago that if his garden could not support more poultry, he would photograph them instead! Rupert's tip for all aspiring poultry photographers is this: 'Understand your breed and be patient – the picture will come.' See his web site at www.rupert-fish.co.uk.

David Bland of SPR, West Sussex, is an acknowledged poultry expert of long standing, and runs an extremely successful business that has won many awards. David has written for a number of magazines, as well as having several book titles under his belt (many of which are also published by Crowood). He has also been involved with videos and DVDs, and is in constant demand as a consultant for books compiled by other people. I am most grateful for his assistance with this project; in particular, for his great kindness in agreeing to read through Chapter 6 'Health and Hygiene', and correct in no small way my elementary errors, which otherwise might have appeared in it.

Thanks too, to David Baird, of Fisher's Farm, Wisborough Green, West Sussex, for giving permission to use the photo of ducks that appears on the cover.

Finally, some information has been gleaned from the Internet, as is the way of modern research. Many web sites include the research of others, and the information contained therein has, I hope, been passed through any copyright procedures. I have, as far as possible, obtained permission to include anything that is directly quotable. If I have omitted anyone, I can only apologize and request that those offended contact the publishers in order that amends may be made in any future reprints of this book.

J.C. Jeremy Hobson

Introduction

What is the difference between domestic waterfowl and wildfowl? No, this isn't a riddle, just something that the newcomer to keeping ducks and geese of any description should realize before embarking further. Basically, domestic waterfowl are the birds we traditionally see around the farmyard, providing eggs, meat and, in some cases, down for pillows and duvets, whereas wildfowl come in a huge range of colourful species that are kept for ornamental rather than productive reasons. The main purpose of this book is to encourage and help those who are interested in domestic waterfowl species; nevertheless, the pleasure of having a decorative and carefully planted pond with some of the most beautiful members of the avian world swimming around on it cannot be overlooked, and it is for this reason that they are given a chapter to themselves.

For the person with a sizable backyard, a pen of ducks is a feasible option, but even the smallest patch of ground can be home to a few ducks provided that the right breed is selected. They will lay a surprising number of eggs, and have the advantage over chickens of not requiring such elaborate housing. As table birds they are fast growers, and a ten-week-old bird may weigh as much as 2.3–2.7kg (5–6lb). Admittedly they can be messy in the really small garden, but even this factor should not preclude the possibility of a few 'bantam' ducks, many types of which will lay almost as many eggs as their large counterparts. Not only are they lovely to look at, they will entertain you with their antics and make perfect 'pets' for adults and children alike. Ducks will eat troublesome slugs and snails as they follow you around the garden, making 'conversation' with you as they do so!

Geese are hardy, virtually disease free, easy to look after and make terrific 'guard dogs'. They will fend for themselves so long as the area in which they are kept has plenty of grass, and even in the winter require nothing more than a simple fox-proof shelter and a few handfuls of grain. Generally kept for their meat (they are one of the most efficient meat producers) and for breeding stock to sell on, they will, nevertheless, lay well during the spring and early summer months. Geese are great if you have the room: a fair-sized lawn, orchard or a small meadow. They are very little trouble and they help control weeds – seven days a week, rain or shine! Their agile necks allow them to pull weeds close to and from within the crop plants and in other situations where a machine or hoe cannot. All of this is accomplished while naturally spreading nitrogen-rich manure. What more could one ask for?

The perfect pair. The gender of ducks is easy enough to distinguish – not least by the curly tail feathers of the male, which are absent in the female (see page 77).

Duckes and Geese

The fairest of the creatures all, shall mayke ye profit seldom small
Be ducks that forage round the cot, for slugges and spillage be their lot,
And supping from the sullen pudge to eat of what we may not judge.
Give without trouble, eggs to eat, or later furnish autumn's meat.
Her final gift the greatest yet, warm fillings for thy coverlet.

And noble is the Roman goose, he'll crop the grasses others loose,
Yet none shall unexpected come when this fine sentry's safe at home.
For puddings that a King would own, her eggs, the finest that are known,
And closed inside the winter barn to dine on spillage harvest corn,
This fatted docile humble beast provides the greatest Christmas feast.

For all the summer they shall lead the scattering fowls upon the mead,
And none shall miss the fallen grain, thy purse it shall not feel the pain,
When safe inside their night roost boxes, warn of devious prowling foxes,
Rain or shine they healthy keep and leave you with untroubled sleep,
The cost of vittals never tall, much profyt be from creatures small.

From *The Cottage Hearth and other Country Poems and Muses*
Philippe de Randolph (1727–1801)

— 1 —
Making a Start with Ducks and Geese

If, in the manner of the popular BBC Radio 4 programme *Desert Island Discs*, I were asked which luxury I would like to take with me on to an isolated archipelago, it would undoubtedly be half-a-dozen geese! Of course I would be not allowed to do so because they are far too practical, offering a supply of eggs, meat and, most importantly, companionship. Companionship? Well, yes, you can never feel lonely when you have a little cluster of geese trotting around after you, all the time being busy and looking important. They are creatures of habit, and often for no reason known to anyone other than themselves, will insist on favouring a certain area and indulging in particular routines. Their human fixation is well known: Conrad Lorentz, the Austrian biologist, discovered their aptitude towards 'imprinting', and much of the fantastic camera work on television showing wild geese in flight has only been possible because of humans taking the place of a young brood's natural parents.

Likewise, a 'bevy' of ducks takes on human qualities – watching them patrolling round the garden in search of slugs and insects, it is easy to imagine them in the persona of old-fashioned headscarf-clad matrons bustling about and doing the rounds of the stalls at a village market, stopping only occasionally in order to mutter disapprovingly amongst themselves about the cost of living. No wonder the character of Beatrix Potter's Jemima in *Jemima Puddle-Duck* is just as popular now as it was a century or more ago when the story was first written.

A BRIEF HISTORY

All of our domestic geese and ducks come from a wild ancestor. In the case of the goose, the European birds are descended from the

11

wild Greylag, from which they differ only in increased size and weight. The Chinese, however, is different in that its ancestor is probably the Siberian Swan Goose. Every breed of duck, with the exception of the Muscovy, can claim their common ancestor to be the common Mallard, or wild duck.

Captive wild ducks were fattened for the table by the Egyptians, Greeks and Romans, and were probably domesticated in China at least 3,000 years ago. Strangely, they were not reared with any serious intent in Europe until perhaps as late as the Middle Ages. As has already been mentioned, the Muscovy is not derived from the Mallard, but is in fact a descendant of the wood ducks of Latin America – an improbable pedigree when one compares the big and, to my mind, ugly black and white Muscovy with one of the smaller and very beautiful modern-day 'tree ducks' such as the Mandarin or Carolina. Whatever its ancestry, the Muscovy had been domesticated and developed as a food-producing bird by the South American Indians centuries before being discovered by European explorers and travellers in the late 1400s.

Perhaps the best known of our English breeds of duck is the Aylesbury, which was at one time so popular that almost every steading in that particular area of Buckinghamshire bred them. In fact so good did their reputation become that, in the mid-1800s, any

Every breed of duck, with the exception of the Muscovy, can claim their common ancestor to be the common Mallard, or wild duck.

white duck would, wherever possible, be passed off as an 'Aylesbury' because the vendor knew that they would realize a premium price.

All over the world there is evidence in the form of cave paintings, of web-footed fowl carcasses found amongst offerings left in prehistoric burial mounds, that geese were domesticated at least 2,000 years before the Chinese began to domesticate ducks. In some civilizations they were closely associated with the rituals of birth and death. Whilst it may have been the Romans who introduced geese to Britain (was there anything for which they were not responsible?), it is generally accepted that, by the Middle Ages, flocks of geese were valued throughout Northern Europe. In France, specific laws were passed by the monarch of the time to ensure that the country would always have a plentiful supply of geese, and as an added incentive, farmers keeping them were accorded special privileges. No surprise then, that many of today's breeds of goose are known by the name of a specific town, area or region.

The goose has always been considered a very useful bird because, like the pig, every part of it can be used. At least until well into the mid-twentieth century its feathers were prized just as much as was its fat, as well as the meat and the liver. The giblets were used for stews of various kinds, and the neck either to make sausages for immediate consumption or salamis that would keep for a long time. The feet, which according to Pliny the Elder were considered a delicacy by his contemporary Messalino Cotta, are still highly sought after today in certain areas of southern France.

In Great Britain, geese were driven to market before the days of any road transport, and thousands of Christmas dinners for Londoners would set out from the country hamlets as early as November in order to ensure that there was plenty of time for grazing the roadside verges on the way. In an effort to protect their feet from damage on the sometimes very long journey, the geese had their feet dipped in warm tar, which would form a solid base against the rough stone surface of roads and tracks.

The time of 'Michaelmas' was also one of the regular quarter days for paying rents and settling accounts, and since this was the time of year when young geese were at their best, farmers would often pay off their debts with a brace or more of spring-hatched geese. A few weeks later, many goose fairs would be held, to which birds would be driven from all parts of the county to be sold. Of all the goose fairs, Nottingham and Tavistock are probably the most famous still in existence, but they are now simply pleasure events without any geese at all.

The goose has always been considered to be a very useful bird, and farmers would often pay off their rental debts with a brace or more of spring-hatched geese at Michaelmas.

MAKING A START

The types of ducks and geese you eventually decide upon are, of course, a matter of both personal preference and their suitability to your topographical situation. There are, however, several constants that need to be considered before you even get to the point of choosing the breeds. I would always advise erring on the side of caution when it comes to breed selection, as it is very easy to get carried away with enthusiasm and end up with a garden full of back-to-back duck pens, or an orchard filled with a motley crew of geese. This, it must be stressed, is only my personal opinion, but I wonder whether it wouldn't be better for the novice to build up slowly with just a single breed and learn as much as he can about that before diversifying into something completely different. The showing of ducks and geese is an increasingly popular pastime, but if you are intending to exhibit your birds, make sure that you visit a few shows before deciding which breed to choose. In fact, whether or not you intend showing, it will still pay you to see as many types of ducks and geese as possible before making the final decision as to which you find most interesting and attractive, and also which suit your particular situation and pocket.

There can be no substitute for picking the brains of a local breeder or a qualified judge of a certain breed in which you are interested, but tread cautiously and explore every aspect before being tempted too far into embarking on a hobby that has an undeniably wonderful way of taking over one's life!

HOW MUCH WILL IT ALL COST?

How long is a piece of string? However, one thing certain is the fact that, because of their less demanding requirements, keeping ducks and geese is a cheaper alternative to keeping bantams and chickens. You could go to the extent (and expense) of constructing a pond, which may well be necessary if you eventually choose to keep ornamental waterfowl (*see* Chapter 8), but normally such a thing is not necessary, and your birds will be just as happy with a clean water supply and a bucket or trough in which they can dip their heads from time to time. So for the basics, you need to consider housing, feeding utensils, and the cost of the birds themselves.

The showing of ducks and geese is an increasingly popular pastime, but if you are intending to exhibit your birds, make sure that you visit a few shows before deciding on which breed to choose.

15

Your birds will be just as happy with a clean water supply and a bucket or trough in which they can dip their heads from time to time.

Housing and Fencing

To protect your stock from predators or from wandering off down the road – geese in particular have a marvellous habit of taking themselves off on 'walk-about' in much the same way as a set of nomadic tribesmen – some form of enclosure will be required. This would normally take the form of a pen carefully constructed of wire netting, fixed securely to stout posts and with the bottom 60cm (2ft) either turned out and pegged, or dug in to prevent foxes from digging under the perimeter wire. In certain situations, a temporary fence of 'flexi-net'-style electrified poultry fencing may be all that is necessary. Where just a trio of ducks is being considered (perhaps in the smallest of back gardens), a small movable house and run will give shelter and security; this is all that will be required unless you are considering breeding at a later date, in which case another coop and run will be needed for the broody and ducklings. A simple ark suitable as a night shelter for ducks and geese can be purchased quite cheaply, but when one considers the need for the addition of secure fencing, the option may not be as attractive as was first thought.

Before deciding exactly what housing and enclosures might suit your particular situation, it will certainly pay to scour the advertisements in the likes of magazines such as *Country Smallholding*, *Smallholder* and *Fancy Fowl*, where you can get an idea of what alter-

Where just a trio of ducks is being considered, a small, movable house and run will give shelter and security and may also prove useful as a broody coop at a later stage.

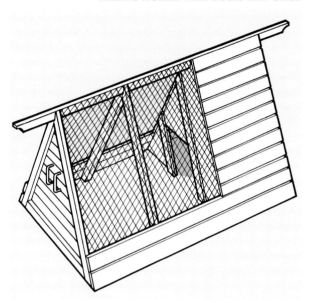

natives are available, together with some up-to-date prices. It might seem elementary, but make sure you understand what is involved when choosing a particular piece of equipment: is it ready to go, or are there any hidden extras? A roll of nylon fencing netting will undoubtedly compare favourably with a roll of good quality galvanized wire netting of the same length, but how much is the electric fencing unit that is necessary to, quite literally, make the whole thing 'tick'?

The Cost of Birds

The cost of birds varies enormously: recent prices paid (at the time of writing, 2009) for three female call ducks were £75.00; a pair of Chinese geese, £100; three Muscovy ducks, £60; a pair of Pekin ducks, £55; and a pair of what were described in the auction schedule as 'farmyard geese' sold for £60. If you are keeping ducks or geese as pets and are not bothered about eggs or breeding, then a pair or trio is all that you need (and they need not be male and female – two or three females will be quite happy running together and do not need a 'man' to keep them in order); but for a regular supply of eggs from a pen of Khaki Campbells, for example, the number of birds required to ensure that regular supply may need to

17

be increased. Again, for the person who is looking out for 'pets' rather than for breeding, the 'pure breed' aspect is perhaps not quite so important, and what should be taken into consideration is whether the birds look healthy.

However, always consider the possibility that you may eventually wish to breed from your stock, in which case you will obviously need to include that all-important drake or gander on your shopping list. To do things in the traditional way, this may necessitate the keeping of a small pen of heavyweight bantams because these can be relied upon to go broody periodically and will, in all probability, make better foster mothers than if you were to try and breed youngsters from their true mothers. Although most geese will successfully rear their own eggs, some ducks are not the best of parents, and a number of breeds, especially the egg-laying types, will almost never go broody. Housing accommodation and the cost of bantams and food will therefore need to be taken into consideration.

Incubators and Sundries

A small incubator might be considered a worthwhile investment, but if you do decide to rear your stock by artificial means, not only will an incubator be required, but so too will some sort of brooding system. For small quantities, these can be quite simple affairs

A pair of Chinese geese can cost upwards of £100 (in 2009).

Leg rings may be necessary for individual bird identification, or as a record of the date of hatching.

involving nothing more than an infra-red dull emitter and a shade, both of which can be bought for £20–£30 (2009 prices), but larger numbers reared will necessitate a more elaborate, and more expensive, system.

Feeding and drinking utensils may be expensive to buy initially, but if carefully chosen, will last a lifetime. Buy the best you can possibly afford, which in most cases means those constructed of galvanized metal. Plastic feeders and drinkers are fine, but no matter what their construction, they tend to have a lesser lifespan due to eventually becoming brittle because of extremes of heat and cold.

And then there are the incidentals such as the regular purchase of suitable floor litter; dummy eggs (to show your ducks where you would *like* them to lay!); leg rings for easy bird identification; membership of your local poultry fanciers' society; and all manner of other things, which, in themselves, are not particularly expensive but should, nevertheless, be considered.

Foodstuffs

At the time of writing there is much consternation regarding the spiralling cost of cereals, which are necessary in the manufacture of compound feeds or given as they are as a 'hard' feed. Wheat prices have doubled in two years because supplies have dwindled as a result of poor harvests and an increased demand for these commodities in places such as China and India where population and income growth have encouraged the production of livestock for their meat. The poultry 'hobbyist' therefore needs to look towards greater efficiency if feed bills are not to preclude his indulging in such activities.

Only keep birds that you can afford to feed: although ducks and geese generally consume less in the way of compound feeds than other types of domestic poultry (especially geese, who will, given adequate grazing during the summer months at least, fend for themselves), there is still a cost to bear in their day-to-day management.

Ducks being kept for their eggs require a balanced diet with adequate vitamins and minerals. If they are free ranging, they will supplement this with any slugs and insects that they find, but even so, ducks will, depending on their size, eat roughly 170–200g (6–7oz) of food per day. Cut down costs by allowing them as much access as possible to places where they can forage and find naturally occurring nutritious greens such as chickweed. If you have a vegetable garden, grow extra crops of lettuce, cabbage and other brassicas, the plants and leaves of which will be appreciated by both ducks and geese when given as an extra 'treat' alongside their afternoon feed of cereal.

Consider whether it is more economical to feed pellets or mash: many keepers of domestic waterfowl feel there is more wastage from feeding mash than there is from pelleted food. Make sure that feeders are cleaned regularly and have no stale food left in them. Waterfowl should, wherever possible, be fed well away from wild birds, and feed troughs placed where they cannot be knocked over and food wasted by being trodden into the litter or vegetation.

The Benefits of being a 'Handyman'

Some costs remain the same – you cannot, for example, practically manufacture your own compound feeds, but other potential expenses can be greatly lessened if you have a little know-how and can turn your hand to DIY. It is no doubt more satisfactory to build your own housing system, but remember that you are unlikely to be able to do so more cheaply than the professional who has tools and 'jigs' at his disposal. However, although it may cost more, you can choose the better quality timber and make a longer-lasting house.

Those of a practical nature can cut costs (without cutting corners) in other ways. An existing shed can be adapted for specific use, and

If you have a little know-how and can turn your hand to DIY, it is no doubt more satisfactory to build your own housing system; but remember that you are unlikely to be able to do so more cheaply than the professional who has tools and 'jigs' at his disposal.

small coops and runs necessary for the rearing of youngstock can be fabricated from all manner of wooden offcuts or redundant rabbit hutches, for example. Being able to build a perimeter fence will definitely prove to be much cheaper than having to employ someone to do the work for you, and having the sense to see what repairs need to be done and being able to act upon what has been noticed, will save a great deal of money over the years.

Regular maintenance is important: refelting a roof on a periodic basis, and replacing any rotting boards or rusting wire netting immediately they are noticed, will ensure that your original house and run last, quite literally, a lifetime. Adding guttering to a large house and funnelling it into a water barrel will help prevent the surrounding area from becoming a quagmire, which, although your ducks and geese might like it, is something no one needs to negotiate on a cold, dark winter's morning. Being able to fix up a lighting system for those dark mornings and evenings is also an advantage, but be sure that your work complies with any regulations regarding electrical DIY.

One word of warning to the handyman: 'invent' what you like in the way of ingenious drinkers made from glass or polythene pipes, but don't ever be tempted to construct feeders from wood – no matter how good your carpentry skills, the nature of wood, and the fact that any joints create minor crevices that are impossible to sanitize, means that you can never fully guarantee that wooden troughs will

21

be free from potential problems when it comes to health and hygiene.

BE PREPARED

Be prepared for the worst! No matter how carefully you pander to your ducks and geese, there will always be potential problems. Disease and illness is always a possibility, and this is discussed in greater depth in another chapter (Health and Hygiene; *see* page 93). Consider the fact that the likes of call ducks or ornamental waterfowl can fly and may require wing clipping or possibly even pinioning. All waterfowl are, to one extent or another, vulnerable to predators: ducks to rats, cats, foxes, mink and hawks; and geese, despite their size, to foxes and the neighbour's wandering dog. The night you forget to shut up the birds is the night that trouble occurs. And don't rely on the carefully constructed little island on the pond – not all waterfowl are bright enough to stay away from the larger bank perimeter!

For poultry being kept overnight in secure houses, it's also possible to fix the pop-hole to work on an automatic timing system. There are several types available, the manufacturers claiming that they take only a few minutes to install. Generally they work on light sensors and are powered by batteries that can sometimes last up to four years. A timing device regulates the hours you wish the pop-hole to close and open. With ducks and geese being notoriously bad

All waterfowl are, to one extent or another, vulnerable to predators.

at going to bed, whilst this system might help to save you worrying on the occasional evening you are away, I personally think it should not be relied upon with any regularity.

PROTECTION FROM PREDATORS

Young birds are especially vulnerable to predation from rats, and it will pay to keep the environs clear of all vermin by the judicious use of poison and traps. Stoats and weasels are also fond of ducks, and stoats especially can cause havoc around an ornamental duck pond where the inhabitants are given more or less free range to roost and nest in the bank-side vegetation. Evidence of their immediate existence is rather more difficult to see than rats: the first sign of any stoats and weasels might be when a kill has occurred. It is possible to keep the area 'trapped' with Fenn traps contained in boxed tunnels, which will prevent your waterfowl from inadvertently being caught, but the subject of setting such traps is rather out of the remit of a book of this nature and your best option is to seek the advice of a local gamekeeper, or to read a gamekeeping/shooting book that deals with such subjects in great detail (*see* the current Crowood catalogue for relevant titles).

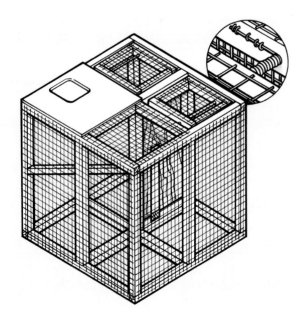

A Larsen trap will humanely capture magpies and crows that may otherwise predate on eggs and young chicks.

23

It is also necessary to be aware of the damage that magpies can cause to both domestic and ornamental waterfowl. Given any opportunity, they will take eggs, and, if your situation is such that they can gain access to young ducks, or even goslings, they will certainly try and do so. Again, it may be prudent to take a leaf from the gamekeeper's book and buy yourself a Larson trap, which can be left set during the spring and early summer when such attacks are likely to be the most devastating. Details of where to purchase, and how to use them can be found on the Internet via search engines such as Google.

KEEPING IN WITH THE NEIGHBOURS

It is unlikely that you will need to gain permission from anyone before you start with ducks and geese, unless you are living in rented accommodation, in which case it pays to check that your landlord has no objection to your acquiring livestock. If you are intending to keep them on an allotment, or to build substantial outbuildings in order to house your stock and equipment, you may need permission from your local council. Some agreements regarding the renting of allotments stipulate that any form of beast or bird cannot be kept there, and buildings over a certain size may be subject to planning permission. For a few ducks and geese this will not be an issue, but keeping on the right side of any close neighbours may be a very different situation indeed!

Ducks are certainly not as noisy as a cockerel crowing at first light, but geese can, unfortunately, make quite a noise, especially if a breed such as the Chinese is chosen. In bad weather both ducks and geese make quite a mess of any damp areas of lawn or garden, and will delight in paddling around in any puddles. As these wet spots become even wetter from the birds' attentions, they can, in warm conditions, become a little smelly – especially when, as will surely be the case, faeces are added to the mix! Much can be avoided by not over-stocking, but even so, you need to be aware of the potential problem if you are to avoid upsetting local human inhabitants. For the same reasons, do not build any pens or keep any birds tight against a dividing boundary hedge or fence.

Also, as much as you may make efforts to avoid encouraging vermin by ensuring that the place is as free as possible of unwanted debris and uneaten poultry food, the very fact that you are keeping ducks and geese will be enough for you to get the blame should even a single rat or mouse be seen in next door's garden. Hopefully

Young birds are especially vulnerable to predation from rats, and it will pay to keep the environs clear of all vermin by the judicious use of poison. Also, the very fact that you are keeping ducks and geese may be enough for you to get the blame should even a single rat or mouse be seen in next door's garden.

your neighbours will be reasonable, but there is always the chance that they may make an official complaint to the relevant environmental authorities, and you may, in the worst case scenario, be forced by court order to get rid of your birds. Avoid potential problems from the very beginning by informing anyone who might possibly be affected or inconvenienced by your intended hobby about your plans, and asking their opinion.

WHEN TO START

There is no right or wrong time to begin keeping ducks or geese, but in an ideal world, the back end of the year may offer the best opportunities to purchase stock. Generally, most fanciers try and dispose of surplus birds in the autumn in order to cut down on the costs involved with overwintering and the problems associated with too many birds on wet ground during the bad weather – it therefore makes sense to buy them in the autumn when prices are cheaper and there is more likelihood of choice. Also, if you were to leave purchasing birds until the spring, much of the early breeding opportunities will be missed whilst waiting for new birds to settle in and for fresh males to mate and eggs to become fertile.

2

Selecting and Purchasing the Right Breeds

The majority of people who consider keeping geese and ducks do so for the pleasure they give, although, as we have already mentioned in the previous chapter, geese can act as superb 'lawn mowers', and some breeds of duck can lay almost as many eggs in a season as many of the commercial breeds of domestic poultry. All types of geese and ducks will lay at least seasonally, and some are excellent meat producers, but it must be said that geese – as compared with other forms of livestock, and cheap to produce as they may be – are not very efficient at converting grass into meat. The likes of the Aylesbury duck, on the other hand, convert their food into meat in the space of a few short weeks and are well worth considering as table birds.

Other types of geese and ducks are bred mainly for exhibition purposes, but there is no reason why any breed should not be shown at either local or national level. Domestic waterfowl are categorized according to their 'weight': thus geese are divided into 'light', 'medium' and 'heavy', while ducks are slightly different in that they are known by the groups 'bantam', 'light' and 'heavy'.

In a book of this nature, which is only ever intended to be an enthusiastically written guide rather than a comprehensive tome, it is difficult to know which breeds to include and which to leave out. Some readers are bound to say, 'Oh, but he's not included the Lesser-spotted, Pink-footed Tree goose!', or some such, for which I apologize; nevertheless, the breeds described are, I believe, the ones most likely to be encountered at shows and exhibitions, or when reading other books concerning the keeping of ducks and geese.

BREEDS FOR EGG PRODUCTION

Ducks

Breeds such as the Khaki Campbell are known to lay as many as 300 eggs in a single season. Like chickens, ducks tend to lay most of their eggs in the early morning and, if given free range, will lay in vegetation before covering their eggs with grass, making them difficult, if not impossible to find. To avoid such problems, it is best to keep ducks confined in their house until about 10am.

The Abacot Ranger

I have included the Abacot Ranger in the egg-laying section because although it is sometimes used as a meat-producing bird, that is very much its secondary role; it is anyway classified as a 'light' breed. It originated in England. The Ranger is only ever seen in the one colour: in the male, the colouring of the head, neck and chest is remarkably similar to the Mallard; the female is basically off-white with flecks of fawn and dark wing feathers.

Abacot Ranger drake.

Bali drake.

Buff Orpington.

The Bali
Originating from Indonesia, the Bali is quite an upright-looking bird and is seen in many colour variations. It has a small crest or 'top knot' at the back of its head. It is becoming increasingly popular amongst enthusiasts looking for an interesting, easily kept bird, and is frequently seen at poultry shows.

The Buff Orpington
This duck has always been known as a *Buff* Orpington because until relatively recently buff was the only colour bred: however, nowadays other colours are being developed, and it would perhaps be more correct to refer to the breed simply as the 'Orpington'. As the name suggests, it was first bred in England (Kent) and is a relatively good egg layer.

The Campbell
Most often seen as the type known as 'Khaki', Campbells can, however, be white in colour, and also in a colour variation that is known by the fancy as 'dark'. Being hardy and good foragers, they make the ideal beginner's duck. Originating in England, they were developed by a certain Adele Campbell, who crossed Indian Runner, Mallard and Rouen ducks in pursuit of a bird that would lay continually throughout the year. As the breed is known to produce 300 or more eggs in a season, it is probably safe to say that she succeeded in achieving what she set out to do!

The Dun and White
What you see in the name is what you get on the bird, and in this one there are no other colour variations! It is an attractive-looking duck, but being of a relatively light build, is more inclined to fly than are some other breeds – this may be a consideration in your choice as it could become embarrassing to be forever collecting your birds from the neighbour's garden! Of course a net over the pen would prevent the problem, or you could clip one wing, but if you did this you would not then be able to exhibit.

The Indian Runner
Known long ago as the 'Penguin duck' due to its original colouring and peculiar stance, it is my experience that the Indian Runner is, rather like the current advertisement for the product 'Marmite', either loved or hated; however, it seems that the former is probably most likely to be the case, as it is second only to the Call duck in being the most popular variety currently being kept as a pet. It is

White Campbell.

Indian Runner drake.

An excellent example of the Magpie breed.

Welsh Harlequin drake.

31

well liked in Britain because it is a hardy forager and a good layer. It is thought to have been first introduced into Dumfriesshire by a ship's captain returning from Malaya in 1876. The Indian Runner was instrumental in the formation of the Campbell, being an important outcross at the time of its development.

Easily recognizable by its tall, upright stature, there are several colour combinations, including black, white, fawn, fawn and white, chocolate, and 'trout'. Runner eggs are larger than those laid by Campbells, which are the same size as normal hen eggs. They are a fascinating breed, and the Indian Runner Duck Association produces regular newsletters with articles on their colour, history and general management.

The Magpie
The black and white colouring makes it obvious why this breed has been given the name 'Magpie', although there is also a blue and white variety. It originated in the UK. Despite being classified as 'light', it is sometimes considered to be dual purpose, producing both eggs and meat.

The Welsh Harlequin
The Welsh Harlequin originated, unsurprisingly, from Wales! The colouring was derived from a 'sport' of the Khaki Campbell, which the breed also resembles in shape, size and weight. The Harlequin was developed by a Group Captain Leslie Bonnet in the mid-twentieth century from a pen of Campbells, and for several years Bonnet referred to them as 'Honey Campbells'.

Geese

Unlike some other types of poultry, the breeding season for geese is short; eggs are laid from about February to late May, laying being triggered by the lengthening days. Even the egg-producing breeds will not lay all the year round, but generally, the 'medium' varieties of geese make good laying birds. One of the best known of the lighter egg-laying types is the Roman; the Chinese are also considered good layers by some fanciers, but most would include that particular breed in the 'exhibition' section.

What they might lack in quantity as far as the numbers of eggs are concerned, geese make up for in quality – goose eggs contain a vast amount of yolk and are therefore very rich and consequently very much an acquired taste. A large goose egg is about the weight of three hen's eggs and makes wonderful scrambled egg, omelettes and, as my grandmother used to do, the most divine egg custard.

The Buff
Both the American Buff and the Brecon Buff are similar in colour, but the American can be identified by its orange bill and legs and its slightly heavier stature, whereas the Brecon Buff is slightly finer in appearance and has a pink-coloured beak and pink legs.

The Buff Back
The Buff Back weighs about the same as the Brecon Buff, but as its name suggests, only its back, thigh parts and neck are buff-coloured; the remainder of the body is white. The beak and legs are orange.

The Chinese
Much the lightest of all the goose breeds, the Chinese (sometimes known as the Knob-fronted or Swan goose) is a very good layer. It also makes a marvellous watchdog; I have kept them for many years, and know from personal experience that they will give warning of the fact that a leaf has just fallen from a tree! In this respect they are as noisy as guinea fowl, and it is as well to bear this fact in

An American Buff.

The Buff Back.

mind if you have very immediate neighbours. They are, to my mind, particularly attractive with their slim body, long elegant neck and the knob at the top of their beak. Perhaps most commonly seen as grey, there is also a white Chinese variety.

Although the Chinese is quite distinct as a species, having a different number of vertebrae in its neck, it will breed quite freely with all other types of geese, and the hybrids produced are fertile.

The Embden
The Embden is dual purpose in that it is both egg layer and meat producer. Along with the Toulouse (with which it is frequently crossed), it is probably the best known and most easily identifiable of domestic geese. It originated in northern Europe. Embdens are big, heavy birds; the pure breds are always white in plumage.

The Grey Back
Also known as the Pomeranian, this attractive-looking goose originated in eastern Germany and Poland. The coloured feathers are darker than those of the Buff Back, but otherwise it is similar in weight and body carriage. Its beak and legs are a darker orange than the Buff Back.

An Embden goose.

The Grey Back or Pomeranian.

The Pilgrim

Bred in the UK, the Pilgrim goose is seen less often nowadays, like the Roman below. This is a shame, because they are attractive birds, and are somewhat unusual in the fact that the male is always white and the female always grey. Because of their genetics, the eyes of the male are blue, whilst those of the female are hazel brown in colour. As a pair, they would undoubtedly look very handsome wandering across a stretch of grass or grazing in an orchard.

The Roman

A good layer – as far as any goose can be – the Roman originated in Europe. It is quite small, and relatively lightweight. With its pure white plumage it might be considered a little boring in appearance, nevertheless it is a very pretty-looking goose, and its characteristics would make it a charming and interesting pet, especially for the first-time keeper. No longer as common as it once was, breeding the Roman would help ensure that it continues to be enjoyed by future generations.

The West of England

Like the Pilgrim (*see* above), the West of England is a traditional breed; another similarity is that the gander is white whilst the goose

The Roman goose is a good layer.

is grey or, nowadays more commonly, grey and white. Old paintings of rural and farmyard scenes in which geese feature are almost certainly depicting examples of this particular breed. There is an almost identical goose in France known as the 'Normande', the male of which, like the West of England, is always white, whilst the female is grey and white. Both varieties are easy to breed.

TABLE BIRDS

Ducks

Ducks intended for the table should be marketed at around ten weeks; keeping them beyond this time may result in a loss of condition, and from a practical point of view they will undoubtedly be more of a problem to pluck due to the new stubbly feather growth. The most common 'heavy' or table breed of duck is the Aylesbury, but the different crosses between many pure breeds are also suitable for meat. There are also 'overlaps' of breeds that suit both meat and egg production; for example, although Pekins are used commercially as table birds, they are also quite good egg producers.

Aylesbury duck.

The Aylesbury
Of the early table ducks, the Aylesbury had no equal, and in the nineteenth century almost all white ducks were known by that name due to the fact that the best came from the Vale of Aylesbury. However, what is known today as a meat-producing Aylesbury has probably had hybrid broiler and Pekin blood introduced into its make-up over the years. The exhibition Aylesbury is very different in appearance to its utilitarian counterpart, although both are always white in colour. The beak should be flesh-coloured; amongst the showing fraternity an orange beak is considered to be a fault.

The Duclair
Sometimes known as the Rouen Clair (but not to be confused with the Rouen breed), the Duclair originated in France where it was very popular as a table bird for many years. It resembles the Mallard slightly, especially in the plumage of the female; there are no colour variations. The legs and beak are also similar to those of their wild ancestors.

The Muscovy
The Muscovy is unique in that it is the only breed not to have descended from the wild duck or Mallard. As anyone who has seen this large, cumbersome bird sitting on a fence or garden pergola will know, they are quite happy perching, whereas all but the ornamental tree ducks, such as Carolinas and Mandarins, prefer to spend their days with their webbed feet well and truly on the ground. They are thought to originate from South America, and were introduced to Britain in the mid-seventeenth century. The meat yield in the Muscovy is higher than in any other duck, with at least 50 per cent more breast meat; interestingly, all the meat is 98 per cent lean, and the skin has 50 per cent less fat than other ducks – making it almost a healthy diet option!

Muscovies are most commonly black and white in plumage, although they can also be found in varying shades of grey and brown. All have a bright red crest around their eyes and above the beak. Left to her own devices, a Muscovy female will sit and successfully brood her eggs. If considering breeding, remember that, unlike other types of domestic duck, their eggs take longer to hatch – thirty-five days as opposed to the more usual twenty-eight. Another interesting point to note is the fact that although the drake will mate with other breeds, the resultant hybrids are sterile.

Pekin
Not surprisingly, given its name, this breed originated in China. It is as popular in America as it is in Britain, although to confuse matters there is also a German variety, which can be distinguished from its American or UK cousins by its much more upright stance. Both types have yellow beaks and orange legs. The Pekin is always white in colour.

The Rouen
The Rouen is sometimes classified as an exhibition bird, but living in France as I do, I know that here, in its home country, it is still very much thought of as a meat producer. Like the Duclair, its colour markings are almost identical to the Mallard, especially on the male. The feathers of the female are more 'chocolatey', and each feather has attractive pencilling. Both male and female are much heavier than the Mallard and possess a very deep-looking body.

The Saxony
The Saxony breed originated in Germany, where it was developed as a table bird. The duck is buff in colour, while the drake

Rouen duck.

Saxony drake.

Silver Appleyard duck.

has a ruddy chest and grey points. Although it might have been bred for its meat, Saxony enthusiasts tell me that certain strains will lay as many as 150 eggs – about half the number expected from the Khaki Campbell, but impressive enough and a good reason to consider keeping a few as pets. It is a quiet bird, with a placid, easy-going temperament, and as such would be ideal for children.

The Silver Appleyard

The Silver Appleyard originated in England and is only ever one colour. The male's plumage very clearly shows its Mallard ancestry, while the female is very attractive in plumage and shape – a typical-looking traditional farmyard duck. They are not, however, very easy to breed true to type, even when hatching eggs from known pure-bred parents – but this is a complicated business and well outside the remit of this book. However, anyone interested in finding out more should read the very informed articles and books written by Mike Ashton and his wife Christine, both acknowledged experts on the breeding and rearing of all types of duck.

Geese

Generally, geese intended for the table are at their best in their first year. Their meat is moist, possessing its own individual and unique taste. Once geese begin to mate or lay, however, the quality of the flesh toughens and never really regains its delicacy. Birds should be produced in the spring for marketing at the end of the same year. One of the heavy breeds of domestic geese that are popular as table birds is the Toulouse, which is often crossed with the Embden.

The Poitou

For many years the Poitou goose was reared as much for its feathers as for its meat. The unfortunate birds would be plucked alive at least four times during their permitted lifespan of approximately seven months – and after slaughtering, they were then plucked for the fifth, and obviously final time. The Poitou originated in the Vienne region of France where it is thought to have been bred for the dukes of Aquitaine by Dutch traders who settled in the area. A medium-sized goose, it is always white-feathered with a yellow orange beak and clear blue eyes. It is not often seen in the UK, but if a source could be found it would make an interesting variety to keep, and due to its history, would no doubt prove a good talking point!

Toulouse female.

Toulouse
The Toulouse was bred in France where it is kept not only for its meat, but also, and perhaps more importantly, for the production of *pâté de foie gras*. The French are both the largest producers of *foie gras* (providing 60 per cent of the world market) and its most enthusiastic consumers – it is they who have established its characteristics and regulated production by passing a succession of laws, none of which could have been done without the aid of the Toulouse goose! It is a heavy goose, and there are no colour variations. It is often described in books and standards as being 'boat-shaped'.

There is also, confusingly, an exhibition Toulouse. More correctly known as the Giant Dewlap amongst breeders, it can be similar in markings to the 'proper' Toulouse, but there are also white or buff strains. It is even heavier than the utilitarian type, and possesses very obvious dewlaps hanging from its throat region.

EXHIBITION BIRDS

Ducks

Any of the duck breeds can, of course, be exhibited and shown at local club level, agricultural shows or at events organized by, or associated with, either the Domestic Waterfowl Club or the British Waterfowl Association; but if you are considering keeping ducks as pets, then why not think about acquiring a few bantam ducks?

Can you have such a thing as bantam ducks? Well, rather like bonsai trees, which are artificially dwarfed versions of the natural stock, there is no reason why any breed cannot in theory be miniaturized, and advertisements for bantam ducks are often seen in the specialist poultry and smallholder magazines. It can be easy to confuse ornamental breeds of duck such as Carolinas and Mandarins with 'bantam' types, purely on account of their small size, but technically these are classified as wildfowl rather than domestic (although the American Bantam Association does actually recognize them in their bantam duck classes). There isn't quite the same scope for choosing a particular type of bantam duck as there is when it comes to selecting a poultry breed; nevertheless, some versions of our domestic duck are very attractive, and it may be possible to find

A fine example of a Blue Swedish duck.

43

bantamized examples of any of the previously mentioned breeds. Species of normal sized ducks that are officially classified as exhibition species are described below.

The Blue Swedish

The plumage of the Blue Swedish (or Swedish Blue) should be basically grey-blue, with a small white bib on both the male and female. Two of the outer primary feathers are also white. Experienced fanciers who breed for show sometimes have to cull quite a few of their bird's offspring due to the fact that quite often undesired colours such as silver, black and brown are thrown. For someone who just wants a few pets, it might be possible to obtain these unwanted colours quite cheaply (or even as gifts), should you have a breeder of Blue Swedish in your area. In the interests of maintaining the standards, you might have to give an assurance that you would not breed from these birds.

Call Ducks

Call ducks are by far the most popular duck to be kept as a pet. Originally referred to in earlier writings as the Decoy, its name changed to the Call at some point in the latter half of the 1880s, when the only known colours were mallard and white. Despite originating in the East Indies, the Dutch long ago realized the value of the Call duck in encouraging native wildfowl to their breeding sanctuaries, from where they could be trapped or shot. Today they are the smallest and most popular of our hobby breeds, as they are very tame and easy to rear. In relation to their size they seem particularly noisy, but that only adds to their character, as long as you are situated far enough away from any neighbours who may complain.

What these ducks lack in laying capacity the females make up for in being superb mothers, and, unusually for most duck breeds, they will brood and rear their ducklings to maturity with very little assistance – but to do so successfully, you may do better in trying to obtain birds that are *not* bred from generations of exhibition stock, as the chances are that they will lay even fewer eggs, some of which may be infertile, or thin shelled; and getting them to hatch (especially in an incubator) can be quite difficult. There are a great many varieties of plumage, the most common being white, but all colours are seen, ranging from apricot to yellow-bellied.

The Crested White

Although mainly seen as white, there are other colours being recently developed, including apricot and silver appleyard. As the name

There are many colour varieties of Call ducks, including silver.

suggests, they have a large crest sitting centrally at the back of the head, and in the show world, the symmetry of this crest is considered most important. Breeding for exhibition is perhaps a little complicated for the newcomer to duck keeping, but when kept purely as pets, there is no reason not to consider this particular breed.

The Cayuga
The Cayuga comes from North America. It is self-coloured with an attractive iridescent 'beetle-green' sheen. The beak (which I suppose I should more correctly describe as a 'bill') is dark slate in colour and the legs are orangey black. If exhibiting, any birds showing too much orange would be marked down by the judges.

Geese

The African
A rare breed in the UK; the African goose actually originated in China, which might explain the similarities to the slimmer and

45

Cayuga duck.

smaller Chinese. Like the Chinese, there is a pronounced knob at the top of the beak. It has in the past been crossed with both Embden and Toulouse geese, and the produce of those crosses were considered to be extremely fertile and profitable. There is a white variety as well as the grey.

Although rare in the UK, that doesn't mean it is absolutely impossible to source, and there are several breeders, some of which may be found advertising in the specialist poultry press, or by contacting either the British Waterfowl Association or the Domestic Waterfowl Club of Great Britain.

The Sebastopol

After the Crimean War, a Russian variety of goose was introduced into the UK, now commonly known as the Sebastopol. This breed differs slightly in that its feathers are singularly elongated and curly on its back and wings, or even curled and twisted all over its body. It is usually kept as an exhibition or 'fancy' breed, rather than for any practical use. From personal enquiries it proved to be very dif-

The African goose actually originated in China, which might explain its similarities to the Chinese breed.

ficult to locate many breeders in the UK. Generally seen as a white plumaged bird, there is also a buff variety.

WHERE TO BUY YOUR STOCK

Having selected the breed that best suits you, the next question is where to locate prime stock. Arguably, the best source is from private breeders who become known to you as a result of joining a local poultry club or visiting shows and exhibitions, or who advertise regularly in reputable magazines. They will have gained a considerable reputation over the years, and will have much to lose by selling poor quality stock. Exercise caution when responding to newspaper adverts or to contacts via a third person. There is no harm in taking someone along with you whose opinion you can really trust, and if the would-be vendor is honest (and most involved in the waterfowl world are!), he or she will certainly have no objection to someone offering a second opinion.

It is nowadays also possible to buy waterfowl, both domestic and ornamental (and indeed most other types of poultry), via the

Internet, but unless the person who is selling is already known to you or your mentor, there is always the risk that you are buying something about which you know nothing. There are often insufficient details posted about how old the birds are, or if attempting to start with eggs, whether these are fertile. A photo showing good specimen examples may even be of birds totally unrelated and unrepresentative of the stock that eventually arrives at your doorstep, so although many sellers on the Internet are undeniably trustworthy and genuine, it pays to treat all with suspicion until all the details can, one way or another, be verified.

Sales and Auctions

Apart from general poultry and domestic waterfowl auctions, there are, from time to time, rare and pure breed sales held throughout the country, some of which are advertised in magazines such as *Smallholder* or *Farmer's Weekly*. There is often a 'show' held before

Sales and auctions are sometimes a good place to purchase your initial stock.

bidding commences, at which the birds to be sold are assessed by an experienced and qualified judge who places the best birds into 'first', 'second' and 'third' in the same way as they would at a conventional show. It is a good way of ensuring that you are buying stock that is, in the opinion of at least one other person, good quality. The resultant bidding prices will of course reflect this. Many club shows and exhibitions include an occasional selling class, and these are also likely to be full of reasonably good quality birds.

Wherever you choose to buy, always be sure to only bid for the birds you have your eye on, and set yourself an upper limit as to how much you want (or can afford) to pay. I know from personal experience that it is all too easy to let your heart rule your head on these occasions, and I have more than once (along with many others, I'm sure) come away from such a sale with stock I didn't need and for which I had no room. Only ever be tempted into paying more than your upper limit if the seller is known to you, and you are sure that it is the only way of ensuring that you go home with excellent quality stock.

There are some tips particularly worthy of mention:

- If there is more than one pen of a certain breed you wish to purchase and they appear to you to be of equal quality, but one is at the beginning of the sale whilst the other(s) are at the end, it may pay to risk holding out for the pens due to come up last. Hopefully, by that time the majority of other buyers will have spent their money or be on their way, and you could end up paying much less than if you had bid at the beginning of the sale. This is not always the case, of course, but it may be a risk you are willing to take.
- At some sales and auctions where there are duplicate pens of a certain breed, the highest bidder of the first pen gets the option to pay the same for the second lot; so were you to decline from bidding on the first batch thinking that your chance will come with a later lot, you might well find yourself out of the equation.
- It is also often the case that a seller will enter two or more pens containing the same thing, and they will mix the quality of the stock so that you are almost forced into buying more birds than you ideally want, just so as to get the best specimens from each pen.

Finally, remember that each auction has its own set of rules and regulations as well as its own rates of commission, which will be added to the amount you eventually pay for your stock.

3

Housing Requirements, Grass Runs and Ponds

Location is all important, and when choosing the site of your poultry unit, it is essential to consider several things. Wherever possible, the front of the shed should be south-east facing so that the occupants get the benefit of the early morning sun, but by lunchtime the front will be shaded from the hottest weather. Constant winds are to be avoided wherever possible, so pick as sheltered a spot as circumstances will allow – though bear in mind that a protected place may be low lying, in which case you are likely to end up with a mud-bath during the wet winter months. All waterfowl must have shelter

In a perfect world, the best location would be an orchard or lightly wooded area, but the average duck or geese fancier is unlikely to have this luxury.

from the blazing sun, otherwise they could quite easily suffer from heat exhaustion. Hedges and trees cool down an area in a heat-wave, and provide shade on the hottest days, as well as a little frost protection in the winter, so include them where you can.

In a perfect world, the best location would be an orchard or lightly wooded area, but the average duck or geese fancier is unlikely to have this luxury. It is, nevertheless, a fact that all types of poultry prefer a sheltered zone because they still exhibit a slight fear of really open spaces due to the fact that their ancestors were more vulnerable to attacks from avian predators in such a situation. Therefore, if it is possible to include a small tree or a bush or two within the 'free-range' area, birds will feel happier and will range more freely.

One of the big advantages of keeping ducks and geese is that their housing can be very simple: they do not require perches, and nest boxes are not absolutely necessary, although it is important that they have adequate ventilation in order to prevent respiratory problems.

HOUSING

Housing for Ducks

Duck housing does not have to be elaborate, but it must be clean and dry with proper ventilation and safe enough to keep the rain out. Basically all that is required is a dry house with a raised floor. As ducks do not roost, there is no need to provide a house of any great height in order to accommodate perches. A 'rabbit hutch'-shaped house need only be around 1m (3ft 3in) at the front, dropping to roughly 75cm (2ft 6in) at the back; but it is even simpler to construct an 'A'-shaped shed. With either design, a little extra height at the eaves will give better air circulation, especially if the ends of the house are not boarded quite to roof level, and instead are merely protected by the addition of strong wire netting or weld-mesh.

The rabbit hutch design should have a door at the front, whilst the 'A' shape more commonly, but not always, has a door at one end. Either way it may pay to fix the door so that it is completely removable, which will help in the weekly clean-out and in keeping the interior smelling more sweetly in warm weather. It has been suggested that a drop-fronted door can double up as an access ramp; ducks, being less agile than chickens, will definitely need some form of ramp, especially if the shed is raised any distance from the floor. In practice, drop-fronted doors are rarely a good

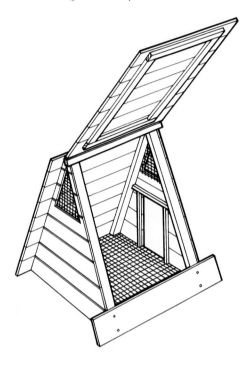

An easily constructed 'A'-shaped shelter suitable for ducks and geese.

idea, as the runners or hinge joints soon become full of debris and refuse to operate efficiently. Probably the best solution is a door that is completely removable, held in place by four 'button' catches.

A house that feels comfortable to the ducks makes shutting them in at night a much easier task, but even so, they will probably need some encouragement most evenings: any shepherding or herding necessary must be done with the minimum of fuss as ducks tend to be more excitable than most other types of fowl, responding best to gentle coaxing and kind words.

Housing for Geese

In reality, geese are hardy enough not to need any housing at all, and they don't seem to mind any of the various weather extremes, except perhaps, as with ducks, they do need protection in the form of shade from really hot weather. Adult birds are, however, and despite their size, a great temptation to foxes, and the goslings a major attraction to rats, so some form of housing will be advisable. It can follow much the same pattern as that for ducks, but obviously the height of the roof or door will require adjusting in order to accommodate the extra height of the birds themselves. Make the ark doors of a mesh that is big enough to allow plenty of air in order to ensure that the geese have adequate ventilation during night-time hours, but small enough to prevent them from pushing their heads through. Of course, stables and outbuildings of any kind can make quite satisfactory housing.

One of the most important reasons for housing geese is to protect them from predators, especially foxes. Geese will, given a routine, soon get into the habit of putting themselves to bed, but neither ducks nor geese are as reliable in this as chickens or bantams.

Flooring

The dirt floors in stabling or existing outbuildings may be used if the soil is light and sandy, but concrete floors are to be recommended, as they are easily cleaned and more sanitary. Provide 0.46sq m (5sq ft) of floor space per bird in the house. In an ark or movable

A house that feels comfortable to the birds makes shutting them in at night a much easier task.

house that is simply used for night-time security, rather than as a place in which your birds will be expected to spend a greater part of the day, the floor should ideally be constructed of wire mesh or slats, rather than solid boarding. This will help the chosen litter to drain, and will also prevent the interior from becoming damp and smelly.

For litter, if the floor is slatted, shavings will be impractical, but straw is a good alternative provided that the top layer is peeled off at least once a week and replaced by fresh. On a solid wooden floor, use wood shavings if you like – they are certainly easier to clean out and do not become as readily matted as straw, and are also more absorbent. Sawdust is not a good idea because of the risk of fine particles causing respiratory problems. To sum up: straw is commonly used, but rapidly becomes wet and soggy, generating a great deal of ammonia; and wood shavings are ideal, but can prove expensive. Despite these factors, never leave your birds without bedding, because they will get dirty very quickly, and may even suffer from what is known as 'wet feather', caused by not being able to keep their feathers cleaned, preened and oiled.

Nest Boxes

Duck and geese eggs have rather porous shells, which means that they all too readily absorb unwanted organisms and taints. Given the opportunity, ducks especially will often lay in or around the edge of a pond or waterway, and eggs found in these circumstances should not be eaten – in the past, the eggs that were casually laid in muddy pens by ducks kept on dirty ponds caused outbreaks of salmonella poisoning in humans. The laying environment must therefore be very clean and, although your birds will probably prefer to lay anywhere bar where they should, nest boxes are, on balance, the best way of ensuring cleanliness.

Nest boxes can be contained within the house because in this way eggs will be kept cleaner, there will be fewer breakages, and no exposure to dampness or sun; whether you can persuade your birds to use the boxes is another matter entirely, but they can be encouraged by putting down a few dummy eggs, which might help to give them the right idea. Boxes should be clean, dry and comfortable, and can be built and placed in rows along the walls. The suitable size for ducks is 30 × 30 × 40cm deep (12 × 12 × 15in), and should obviously be proportionately larger for geese – approximately 50cm (20in) square, with a 15cm (6in) retaining board at the front to hold the nest litter in place.

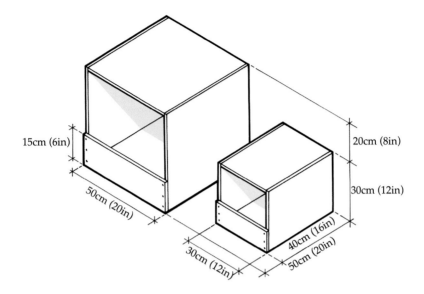

Nest boxes should be clean, dry and comfortable.

Material such as shavings, sawdust or sand should be placed to a depth of 7cm (3in) as a base litter. If you wish to include nest boxes, keep them simple – you may find that the birds will just lay in the straw litter anyway, and given the opportunity, would certainly much prefer to form their own nest in some sequestered part of the garden or outdoor run.

Regular Maintenance

Even though the housing need not be as elaborate as may be necessary for other types of poultry keeping, what you have should be regularly maintained, and its outer surfaces protected from the elements. When I was young, it was a regular autumn task to give all poultry houses a 'once over' with creosote in order to help protect the timbers and to kill off any parasites and mites that may have found homes in the nooks and crevices throughout the warm summer months.

Perfect though creosote was for this job, any avian inhabitants had to be moved to another place until the preservative had dried, and the not inconsiderable fumes had dissipated. After concerns regarding its effect on the user's skin, and its possible potential to cause respiratory problems, this marvellous coal tar-based substance became subject to EU legislation, resulting in restrictions in 2003, and more discussion in 2007; a total ban on its use is likely in the very near future. However, other wood preservatives are available, and although undoubtedly more expensive than creosote, they should be used on a regular basis to protect your housing. Use the time spent doing so to check out any repairs that may be necessary, and don't hesitate to replace a nail, loose screw or hanging hinge before a simple five-minute job becomes one of major proportions.

GRASS RUNS, ORCHARDS AND PASTURE

There can be no picture more typically rural than that of a happy band of ducks waddling their way homewards after a leisurely time spent dabbling in the pond or stream, or of a flock of geese grazing under the fruit trees of an orchard. Grass is the natural food of geese, and great savings in 'artificial' feed can be made by providing good pasture throughout the growing period. Although ducks

There can be no picture more typically rural than that of a happy band of ducks waddling their way homewards after a leisurely time spent dabbling in the pond or stream.

are not grazing birds in the same way as geese, the more space you give them outdoors, the happier they will be, and the less likelihood there is of the run becoming wet and muddy. Like geese, they do appreciate *some* naturally occurring green feed, and their health will also benefit if they can dash around in their search for insects and grubs. Be certain that any pasture or land on which you decide to site your run has not recently been subjected to any chemical treatment that would be harmful to the birds.

As when keeping all types of poultry, a rotation system is to be recommended; if the house is a permanent fixture, try and construct an arrangement whereby it is possible to have at least two outdoor pens running from it; in this way, your birds can be spending time in one whilst the other is recovering. Four pens are even better, and will not cost that much more to construct because it is simply a question of dividing your original two by means of a fence.

Fencing

Keeping ducks and geese in is a simple matter – keeping predators out is not. Unlike an outdoor run to contain chickens and bantams,

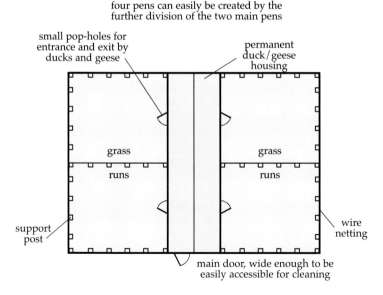

If the house is a permanent fixture, try to construct an arrangement whereby it is possible to have at least two outdoor pens running from it.

When building the gateway, make sure that the method used to fasten it is a secure one. Don't forget to make the gate wide enough to allow for the passage of wheelbarrows or any broody coops and runs that may be needed in the future.

where the height of the fence would need to be at least 1.5m (5ft), the fence surrounding ducks and geese does not need to be very high, since the birds seldom fly. To protect against foxes and even wandering dogs, the fencing surrounding permanent poultry buildings should be around 2m (6ft 6in) high, with at least 30cm (1ft) dug into the ground (or turned out and pegged) to prevent anything from scratching underneath it. Ordinary galvanized chicken wire is perfect for the job, but make sure that it is of good quality – it will be more expensive than the cheap imports readily available, but it will last twice as long. Strain the tops and middle sections with a length of galvanized wire stapled to the posts (but do not hammer the staples right 'home', or they will pinch the wire and cause it to break), and leave the top of the wire netting slightly floppy so that it is more difficult for an unwanted animal to climb in.

Use strong posts; angle-iron ones with holes drilled at appropriate heights to allow a length of straining wire to be threaded through work well and will last a long time, but most people tend to use wooden stakes, which can be obtained either from your local agricultural suppliers or a nearby wood-yard. Make sure they have been pressure-treated with a preservative. Now this was a situation where, in past times, creosote was extremely useful (*see* 'Regular Maintenance' above, page 55): despite its disadvantages around the poultry shed, it was absolutely perfect for preserving the fence posts used to hold up the wire netting of a chicken run. Well soaked in creosote, the life of these posts would be increased three-fold – and the fact that for many years British Rail treated their wooden sleepers with creosote bears testament to its being the best preservative available.

When building the gateway, make sure that the method used to fasten it is a secure one. A central bolt often seems safe, but a determined fox or neighbour's dog pushing and scratching at its base could force an entry. Also, be sure to make the gate wide enough to allow for the passage of wheelbarrows or any broody coops and runs that may be needed in the future.

A nylon net to cover a small outside run can be a useful addition; it should be kept taut by being held up with stakes, though be sure to place an upturned plastic plant pot on the top of each, otherwise the stake will eventually rub a hole in the nylon mesh. With the current worries regarding avian flu, a net is definitely recommended and will go a long way towards preventing the droppings of wild birds falling into the run and possibly infecting your birds.

Electric Fencing

Rather than going to the expense of a high and unnecessarily expensive galvanized fence around your runs, you could construct a simple wire-netting fence of only about 1m (3ft 3in) in height in order to keep your stock where you want them; then to give them additional protection from outside interference, place a temporary fence of 'flexi-net' some distance away. Basically, 'flexi-net' is a nylon fence constructed in squares (in much the same way as traditional galvanized stock fencing), through which strands of wire have been woven; it usually comes in 50m (165ft) rolls. The fence is then connected to an electric fencing unit and a pulse current is passed through it, giving anything that touches it a shock similar to that experienced if one were to contact the single strand fence as used to contain cattle.

In fact it is possible to do away with the galvanized wire-netting fence completely and use the 'flexi-net' to keep your stock in and predators out, but I have tried this with geese, and unless they are somehow taught not to keep pushing against it, it's my experience that they can find their way underneath it. The place I used it was, I must admit, in a confined area, and perhaps if such a fencing technique were used to surround a small paddock or orchard, for example, the situation might be different. Gamekeepers use a double strand of electric fencing around the base of their pheasant release

Wherever any type of electric fencing is being used, it is absolutely imperative that no grass or vegetation is allowed to come into contact with it.

pens in order to protect their birds from foxes, and this system may also be of value to the person keeping ducks and geese.

Wherever any type of electric fencing is being used, it is absolutely imperative that no grass or vegetation is allowed to come into contact with it otherwise it will cause a short and make the fencing far less effective, or it will even fail to work at all.

WINDBREAKS AND BAFFLE BOARDS

Despite the fact that ducks and geese are hardy, in particularly bleak areas, or indeed in corners of the garden where you might wish to see your birds, but the neighbours do not, it may pay to construct some sort of screen as protection. I cannot stress enough the effectiveness of the various types of windbreak material bought at any decent garden centre. Because of its intended use it is always attractive to the eye, can be purchased at a suitable height and length, is simple to erect and, if the right type is chosen, will last for several years. More expensive but equally effective are panels made either from interwoven 'larch-lap' or from hazel – though whatever choice is made, make sure that, when you erect them, you are not putting them so close to the poultry fence that you are, in effect, making it even easier for predators to use your construction as a ladder.

You may also need some baffle boards in a situation where you are housing pens of breeding birds side by side. Without them, the ganders or drakes may be more interested in pacing up and down the pen wire and attempting to attack each other than they are in spending the necessary time with 'the ladies'. A sheet of corrugated tin is probably the cheapest and easiest solution, but it doesn't look very pretty unless painted with animal-friendly paint in a subdued 'country' colour. Boarding is the best, but it is expensive. Again, a good compromise can be reached by using the woven or frond-type windbreak bought in a length from your local garden centre; this filters the wind rather than stopping it dead (so it is less likely to be damaged in a sudden gust), and also prevents the occupants of neighbouring pens from seeing each other.

PONDS AND SWIMMING PLACES

Many people dream of having a swimming pond for their ducks and geese. Although it has been stated elsewhere that a pond is not essential, if a 'paddling pool' can be provided it will help ducks and

You may well need baffle boards in a situation where you have pens of breeding birds side by side. Boarding is the best, but expensive.

geese keep their eyes and vents clean, and it also helps the mating procedure in some breeds. In hot weather, static water can turn green very quickly, hence the need to ensure that any pond or pool is easy to drain unless it is supplied by a constant flow of running water; and in the latter case, you must consider whether a small duck might be able to squeeze out of the outflow or the inflow. Also, will such an arrangement make it easier for predators to gain access?

Making an artificial pond for ducks and geese is not difficult, but it ought to be fitted with some form of drainage and cleaning system. Although the initial outlay will be more than purchasing a length of butyl liner, it will almost certainly last longer and will look more attractive. To prevent the edge of the pool from becoming muddy, you could use cement, or surround the pond with pea shingle, though be sure that whatever material is used will not damage the birds' feet. The surround should extend some distance from the edge of the pond. If the pool is kept full of water, there should be no problem in birds getting out wherever they like, but it is probably a good idea to include a few steps constructed of breeze blocks or bricks submerged just under the water.

Although beneficial, swimming water is not essential for domestic ducks and geese.

— 4 —
Feeding

If this were a book dealing with any other type of poultry, the chapter on feeding would perhaps be one of the longest. As it is, the feeding and general nutritional care of both ducks and geese is so easy that it may well end up being the shortest!

Although ducks and geese have much in common with each other, their actual feeding 'mechanism' is different in several ways. Most significant is the difference in the goose's head, which is smaller and more compact in relation to its body than that of the duck, and its beak is deeper than it is wide at the base, and has a cutting

The upper jaw of the goose has developed in such a way that the lateral edges of the bill (lamellae) have become slightly saw-toothed in appearance, thus enabling the goose to chew the plants that it eats.

In the duck, these same edges (lamellae) have not developed, and still retain their original function, acting more as a filter serving to strain out particles of food and plankton.

edge that is ideal for grazing leaves, grass, shoots and small plants. Over thousands of generations, the upper jaw has developed in such a way that the lateral edges of the bill (the lamellae) have become slightly saw-toothed in appearance, thus enabling the goose to chew the plants that it eats. In the duck, these same edges (lamellae) have not developed into any sort of 'chewing' or grazing mechanism, and retain their original function, acting more as a filter to strain out particles of food and plankton.

FEEDING OUTDOORS

Now here's a tricky one! Normally, in the current climate of bio-security concerns resulting from the (it must be said, sometimes media-hyped) worries of avian influenza, poultry keepers are always encouraged to feed their birds indoors, or at least somewhere where it is less easy for wild birds (known carriers of the disease) to gain access. With ducks and geese, the fact that they spend less of their time in their overnight accommodation makes life difficult. It might be possible to feed your birds indoors twice daily by providing food in the evening once they are shut in, and again in the morning before they are let out, and fortunately ducks and geese will feed at night, unlike chickens, and so will take advantage of food left in the house. Sometimes, however, there may be no alternative but to feed outdoors.

There are certain advantages to feeding outside as far as the fancier is concerned, not least of which is the fact that it reduces the mess created in the house – both ducks and geese like to 'water down' their food, and the passage between feeder and drinker can very soon become soiled. A handful of mixed hard corn can be scattered outside and will very quickly be hoovered up, but in situations where it is desired that birds are fed ad lib – when rearing ducks for the table, for example – there is sometimes no alternative but to feed outdoors, in which case the food needs protecting from the elements.

FEEDING CONCENTRATES

Feeding waterfowl is, as has already been mentioned, as simple as their housing. They will thrive on a basic diet of crumbly wet mash and a separate feed of grain in the evening, but beware of providing more mash than the birds can eat in one session because moist mash will quickly become stale and sour, especially in warm weather. There is no reason why poultry pellets should not be used, but the ideal is a well balanced waterfowl or game-bird ration. If using a feed not specifically intended for domestic waterfowl, ask your supplier's advice and make sure that the feed is suitable for ducks and geese. Assuming that the poultry keeper will acquire youngstock rather than mature birds, it makes sense to begin this chapter by discussing foodstuffs suitable for ducks and geese from hatching through to the age of six weeks, and then from six weeks to maturity.

From Day-Old to Six Weeks

Once your goslings and ducklings have hatched, one option is to feed them for the first four weeks on ordinary chick crumbs, which you can buy in small quantities from any good pet shop. However, be certain that the feed you are using contains only those additives approved for ducks and geese, because certain types of drugs that are sometimes included (anti-coccidiostats, for example) are harmful to young waterfowl, causing lameness or even death. In fact, be very wary of feeding young waterfowl medicated chick crumbs of any kind unless you really cannot get anything else: on balance they will consume greater quantities than the chicks of chickens and bantams, and therefore could possibly ingest too high a dose of the medication, which can be lethal.

If you have only a few ducklings or goslings to rear, they will do very well by being fed a cereal-based dog food, which should be mashed into a shallow saucer with a little water combined. Hardboiled eggs crumbled and added to food in the first couple of days will often encourage newly hatched birds to begin feeding, especially if they are with a broody hen, which will show them what to do. Even incubator-hatched and therefore brooder-reared youngsters that have no mother to guide them will soon begin to peck at the food provided. For the first day or so it is best to cover the brooder base with a hessian sheet rather than wood shavings so that the chicks can only pick up food, and not floor litter. Hessian is ideal because it gives a purchase for their feet; newspaper or similar is too slippery and could result in damaged or deformed legs.

From about three to four weeks of age until feathering, the young birds should be fed grower pellets, which again can be obtained from a pet shop or agricultural supplier. The protein levels contained in the food should by this time have dropped from about 18 per cent down to 16 per cent. If artificially reared ducklings cannot be given access to a grass run at this stage, they will appreciate the addition of fresh greens to their diet; small quantities of freshly cut grass or chopped dandelions are ideal.

Young birds require a different diet to adults, and are best fed little and often when circumstances allow.

Six Weeks to Maturity

The regime for feeding table ducklings remains the same as for any other type of young duckling, but for the last fortnight or so they should be given finisher pellets or mash. If you are aiming to fatten geese for the table, they are perhaps best kept semi-intensively and fed on concentrates for the whole of their lives, when they will very quickly reach market weight.

For birds that are being brought on to join the flock, it is simply a matter of weaning them off grower pellets and on to the pellets or mash that has been chosen to keep them in good condition. If you are keeping ducks for laying, do not be in too much of a hurry to put them on to layers' pellets before they reach point of lay, because this can cause the reproductive organs to mature before the body of the bird. Begin introducing cereal grain a little at a time – at first duck-lings and goslings may pick it up and drop it, but they will very soon identify it as food, especially if there is a parent bird ready and willing to show them what to do.

FEEDING ADULT BIRDS

It should not be necessary to feed adult geese at all during the spring, summer and early autumn months, provided they have access to as much short, sweet grass as possible. Large strains of growing geese will, however, require at least 500g (1lb) per head of mixed grain and pellets per day if their grazing is at all restricted; nevertheless, if supplementary feeding can be kept to a minimum, it will benefit both the birds and your pocket. Ducks can be given pellets or mash in the morning, and then a scattering of wheat or mixed grain in the afternoon.

If you are considering breeding from your stock in the spring, then Christmas-time is not too early to begin feeding a breeders' ration to selected birds – at the very latest it should be included six weeks before the first eggs are required for hatching. If, for one reason or another, it is impossible to source breeders' pellets or mash, then try and obtain a layers' ration containing a protein content of around 17 per cent.

The addition of a little cod liver oil and a small amount of fish-meal may also help improve the hatch rate of eggs, especially during the early part of the year. Probably the easiest way to administer this is to mix it with the afternoon scratch feed of mixed corn, as the oil will help the fishmeal adhere to the grain. Pure white fishmeal provides heat and energy, and small quantities can be given in preference to maize. Unfortunately, it is, I think, impossible to buy in small amounts, but one way round the problem could be for a poultry club or smallholders' society to buy a large bag and split it, and so also the cost, between its members.

Cereals

Cereal grains provide a ready and economic source of energy, and a portion of the bird's protein needs – usually about 45 per cent of the total crude protein requirement. Wheat and barley are the most commonly fed grains, and although barley is the cheapest, wheat is preferred. Kibbled maize is more expensive and maize of any type should not be given too frequently or in too great a quantity due to the fact that it is very fattening and could, if given in excess, cause problems with breeding birds. It is, however, very useful in keeping birds warm during the winter and in boosting egg yolk colour. Too high a proportion of cereal can also lead to protein and vitamin deficiencies, so a correct balance between this and other food sources is most important. If you choose to feed cereals by giving it as a 'scatter' feed, just give as much as will be eaten up in a 20–30 minute period.

It should not be necessary to feed adult geese at all during the spring, summer and early autumn months provided they have access to as much short, sweet grass as possible.

Greenstuffs

Geese will not thrive on coarse, long grass, however much they have access to. Without additional feeding, young birds can quite literally starve to death on such pasture, whereas older birds will eat mostly grass seed. Geese kept off grazing land must be given plenty of cut greenstuffs. Young ducks and geese can be given lawn clippings or even a few turfs of short grass if necessary. If you have a productive vegetable patch, both will much appreciate lettuce that has 'bolted', but it should be chopped for young birds. Fresh duckweed is also important for many waterfowl – fresh enough to contain all the little living animals such as tiny molluscs and larvae as the perfect dietary supplement.

Tit-Bits

Confined birds will benefit from being given a few extra treats, as they are unable to range freely and thus supplement their diet. Earthworms, mealworms, slugs and peanuts are all eagerly devoured – though beware of a fungus that can sometimes be found in badly stored peanuts, which can affect the health of ducks

Free-range ducks find 'tit-bits' in the most unlikely places!

in particular and poultry in general. Cooked vegetables and brown bread are also appreciated, and do not forget a regular supply of mixed grit, as penned birds are obviously unable to source their own.

GRIT

Grit should be available from the age of one week, and after about a fortnight, young birds can also be given crushed shell, for the sake of good bone formation. Layers need a shallow box of limestone grit, or oyster shell. It is also essential to provide plenty of sand and grit to geese so that the gizzard can function properly. Gizzard grit is of course a necessity at all ages, and although it might be supposed that free-range birds will find their own, there might not be sufficient of the right type available, so it may still pay to provide a bought-in supply on a regular basis.

FEEDING AND DRINKING UTENSILS

Feeders protected from the weather by a built-in canopy are good, but expensive, and they still allow access to wild birds. Open troughs, whilst not advised, are nevertheless the most common alternative used by waterfowl enthusiasts, though any pellets or mash contained therein need some sort of overhead covering. The simplest solution is to erect a static feeding shelter made of four short posts and a sheet of corrugated tin, but to do so only encourages birds to one point, which will soon become a stinking, stagnant mess. It is therefore far better to devise a portable feeding shelter that can be moved from place to place on a daily basis. Ducks and geese, being hungry creatures, will quite happily accept a, quite literally, 'movable feast' as part of their routine.

Ducks and geese do not need any specialist feeding equipment, and anything that is suitable for other types of poultry can be used. Where possible, use feeders that allow limited access to the trough, otherwise there will be much wastage, and vermin will be encouraged. It may be worthwhile considering self-feeding hoppers, normally used by game farmers and gamekeepers; these are weatherproof, and have the added advantage of keeping birds amused over a longer period of time because they have to peck at a pendulum device at the base of the hopper in order to obtain their food.

Surprisingly, water has the potential to cause problems in some aspects of domestic waterfowl rearing. The drinker for both goslings and ducklings must not be too deep, as they are notorious for 'playing' in water, and by doing so can suffer from chilling and may even die. If the gap at the base of the drinking fountain is too wide, birds may get in and actually drown, so if a narrow-based fountain is unobtainable, it is advisable to place pebbles, a length of hose or even marbles around the base to prevent full access; this should go a long way towards preventing any deaths.

Although swimming water is not absolutely essential for waterfowl, ducks and geese need to be able to immerse their heads completely to clean any blockage of their nasal passages caused by dirt and food. They also need fresh, clean drinking water, and drinking containers should be kept shaded at all times. Water is best given in troughs or fountains into which the ducks cannot have access, otherwise they will just treat it as a pond. It needs to be supplied in both the house and run, because unlike other types of poultry, ducks will eat and drink at night. It must also be changed regularly, or it will quickly become fouled. Ducks of all breeds like to eat and drink alternately, and often actually dunk their food in the water before eating. To prevent damp litter, stand the water container on a flat wire-netting platform raised on battens.

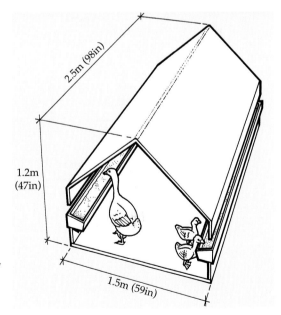

Open troughs, whilst not advised, are nevertheless the most common alternative used by waterfowl enthusiasts; any pellets or mash contained therein need some sort of overhead covering.

It may be worthwhile considering self-feeding hoppers, which are weatherproof and keep birds amused over a longer period of time because they have to peck at a pendulum device at the base of the hopper in order to obtain their food.

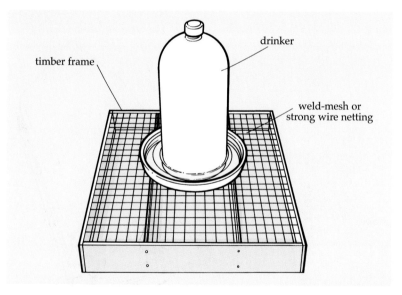

To prevent damp litter, stand the water container on a flat wire-netting platform raised on battens.

Where geese and ducks do not have access to a pool or stream, it is advisable to move drinkers to a new location each day: if they stay in the same place, the land around them can rapidly become overgrazed, muddy, and filthy with droppings, particularly during the winter season.

STORING FOOD

It is important to obtain fresh feed, and it should be stored in covered containers with tightly fitting lids in a clean, dry, cool area away from other animals and vermin. Always buy your food from a busy store that is known to have a good turnover of poultry products: this way there is less chance that you will be buying stock that has gone stale or even beyond its 'sell-by' date. Feed stored longer than eight weeks is subject to vitamin deterioration and rancidity,

Ducks and geese do not need any specialist feeding equipment, and anything that is suitable for other types of poultry can be used. Feeders protected from the weather by a built-in canopy are good, but expensive, and they still allow access to wild birds; where possible, use feeders that allow limited access to the trough, otherwise there will be unnecessary wastage.

When You Go Away

One of the problems of keeping livestock of any kind is the fact that it can sometimes be difficult to get away as a result, and for the waterfowl fancier with a young family who is obliged to take their break during the school holidays, it can be something of a logistical nightmare. Nothing is impossible, however, and it's probably better to go along with family plans rather than risk your partner's cry: 'You think more of those birds than you do of me and this family!' And even if this may be the case, it's probably best not to admit to it!

So, what can be done? If you have kind neighbours with an interest in your hobby, you might be able to come to a mutually beneficial arrangement: with the promise that they are welcome to the eggs, or that you will look after their greenhouse/budgie/pet mountain lion or whatever when they next go away, it is perhaps not too much of an imposition to ask them to feed and generally keep an eye on your stock while

If you have kind neighbours with an interest in your hobby, then it is perhaps not too much of an imposition to ask them to feed and generally keep an eye on your stock while you are absent.

you are absent. You should, of course, spend a fair amount of time explaining your routine and ensuring that they understand what is being asked of them.

Make the job as simple as possible for those who are keen and enthusiastic, but have no personal experience of your hobby. You may find it worthwhile to 'colour code' your feed bins, or at least to identify the contents of each by attaching a label or writing on the lid with paint or an indelible felt pen marker. I know of several poultry owners who use plastic bins kept inside the shed or outhouse that have been bought in different colours specifically to aid instant identification – blue for growers' pellets, red for chick crumbs, green for layers', and so on. They claim that not only does it make it easier for their neighbours when asked to look after stock, but it is also useful to the owners themselves when they venture out to feed on a Sunday morning after a heavy Saturday night!

especially during the summer months. Any cereal or seed bought as a 'treat' for the birds (peanuts, linseed and the like) must be clean and shiny in appearance and should not smell musty or contain any dust.

The temperature and humidity of the place you store your food is also important, as is the need to keep the area clean, well lit and ventilated with fresh air. Store bags on a pallet so that air can circulate all round them, and keep their edges well away from the walls, especially if these are tin, brick or concrete where moisture and condensation are likely to be a problem. The backyard poultry keeper whose land allows him to keep a fair number of birds and therefore needs to buy in bulk should take care not to store more than ten bags on each pallet.

It is a good idea to design the storage area to facilitate the FIFO ('first in, first out') system, where bags are stored in consecutive order so that the oldest can be withdrawn first – it is too easy to empty the place nearest to the door, then replenish that space with 'fresh' food and use that first again, leaving older bags at the back of the building to go stale.

Check that the contents of each bag are clearly marked, and that all possess the paper label stitched into the bag when packed – it contains vital information such as the date of manufacture, the percentage level of individual ingredients, any drugs included and, perhaps most important of all, the expiry date.

5

Breeding, Hatching and Rearing

Unless you intend to buy new, unrelated stock for ever (and why do that when you can breed your own), there will come a time when circumstances and personal enthusiasm dictate that you will want to rear your own birds. You can, in certain situations, leave a goose to sit her own eggs and she will do so quite successfully, but there are many other occasions where you will want to place a particular male with a group of females in order to develop a strain of your own. Also, some strains of duck are not the best natural

Although water is not essential when breeding ducks and geese, mating in the wild is almost always carried out on water and the fertility of most types of waterfowl will undoubtedly be improved if they, too, have access to water for mating.

mothers, and you may need to give nature a helping hand by selecting the most fertile eggs and sitting them under a broody hen or in an incubator.

Fortunately, unlike some other forms of poultry, breeding ducks and geese is not too complicated, but, having mentioned elsewhere that water (other than that for drinking and cleanliness) is not essential when keeping ducks and geese, mating in the wild is almost always carried out on water, and the fertility of domestic ducks will undoubtedly be improved if they, too, have access to water for mating.

MANAGING THE BREEDING PROGRAMME

Selecting Birds for Breeding

The main factor in the selection of breeders is bodyweight, and since this is inherited, birds should only be selected when they have reached maturity, as only then is it possible to choose birds that are a typical weight according to their breed standard. There are, however, several other aspects to consider, not least of which are body conformation, correct feathering, the known egg-producing qualities of parents, and the likely fertility and hatchability of a particular strain. Potential breeders should also be uniform in size as well as weight.

To tell the gander from the goose might be difficult in some strains of geese, and only the pure-bred Pilgrim and West of England can be accurately sexed due to the completely different colouring between male and female. In most situations, an overall general appearance is all one can go by, the gander being slightly larger and heavier than the goose. In some breeds the male may have a louder call, and sometimes the hint of a 'crown' on the top of the skull. If your birds are the type that will come and 'tell you off' when you enter the paddock or orchard, and if it is always the same bird in the lead when doing so, then it is a reasonable (but by no means definite) assumption that you are being greeted (or warned off) by the male! Experienced geese keepers can tell males from females by inspecting a bird's vent, and there are some who maintain that geese can be sexed by the number of folds of skin hanging down between the legs.

Ducks are far simpler to sex, both because the feather coloration is generally different between male and female, and also the drake will have a rounded curly feather in the centre of the parson's nose.

It is not always easy to sex geese from just looking at them.

Age at Which to Breed

If you have acquired older stock as a result of your initial interest in domestic waterfowl, you can still achieve some success, but in an ideal world, you should not use birds that are more than about six years old as far as ducks are concerned, and perhaps eight years for geese (geese will live beyond teenage years). After such times, females are less productive, and the quality and viability of the eggs you do collect will begin to decline.

Similarly, never rush into using very young stock even though, from their daily activities, they might seem sexually mature. Two-year-olds in both ducks and geese are better breeders than younger birds, and it is certainly a fact that one should never mate any birds that are under six months of age. This is especially important in table breeds where it might reasonably be assumed that size is wanted, and size is easily lost by using small eggs from first-year female birds. Males, on the other hand, have a longer breeding life, especially those of the light breeds.

Mating

Professional breeders would select and create a breeding pen, but any newcomer will, in all probability, be restricted in what stock they have available to breed, and in nine cases out of ten, their entire pen will prove to be the nucleus of their breeding programme. However, in an ideal world, this is what should happen!

Ducks
The number of ducks that a drake can mate with depends on the size of the birds. With light breeds, one drake to ten ducks is fine, whereas with the heavier breeds it is one drake to five ducks; on average, however, it is safe to assume one drake to five to eight ducks.

Be aware that some drakes can become very aggressive towards their females during the breeding season. This problem is more likely to occur when there is competition between males, either in the same pen or when they are kept next door to each other.

Unlike geese, ducks make very poor mothers, and it is advisable to collect and hatch fertile eggs under a broody hen or in an incubator.

The number of ducks that a drake can mate with depends on the size of the birds.

Geese

It is interesting to note that geese are monogamous in the wild, but polygamous when reared as farm birds. For maximum fertility levels, the ideal ratio is one male to every three or four females, and it is important that they are all introduced at the same time; bringing in a bird at a later date will sometimes result in the newcomer being ostracized and ignored. Unlike ducks, where the drake will mate with a female at first sight, a gander will not always mate until he has become settled with his 'harem', and so it is essential that they are kept together for at least five to six weeks prior to the time when any fertile eggs are required.

The goose makes an excellent mother – unlike the female of the duck species – so it is possible to leave her to brood her own eggs and look after the goslings once they are hatched. Given the opportunity she normally makes her own nest outside, though if confined she is not averse to sitting happily in a quiet corner of the shed or night shelter. It is not unknown for females to share the same nest, and in such a situation it is advisable to mark the eggs on which one goose may be actually sitting with a heavy pencil mark: in this way any freshly laid eggs (which will obviously be unmarked) can be collected and removed, leaving only the ones to be hatched remaining.

Provided that the area contains short-cropped grass and there are not too many obstacles in or behind which young goslings can get trapped, there should be no problem in leaving a mother goose in her own environment once her clutch has hatched. Any other geese tend to become doting 'aunts', and the gander a proud, protective and attentive father. They will, however, require some supplementary feeding such as chick crumbs or mash – and this can get quite expensive, as it will not be long before the rest of the 'family' also pitches in!

Management of Breeding Birds

Breeding birds should not be too fat when they begin to lay; any tendencies towards becoming overweight can be avoided by maintaining those birds selected for breeding on a maintenance ration until about six weeks before the first eggs are required for hatching. At this time birds should be fed breeders' pellets or mash, which should contain about 16 per cent protein. Although every effort should be made to keep nesting areas as clean and hygienic as possible, it is particularly important to do so when intending to pick up the eggs for incubation, in order to prevent any unwanted bacteria from finding their way through the extremely porous shells.

Collecting and Storing Eggs
Collect eggs as many times daily as is practicable, as this will help to keep the shell in good condition and avoid any hairline cracks. A regular collection also helps to prevent eggs overheating in the warmer months. Mark in pencil the date on which the egg is laid on the shell so that you can be sure that only the freshest eggs are set. Only perfect eggs should be considered for hatching, so do not include any that are misshapen, cracked or the wrong colour, and whose shells are chalky or lumpy in appearance or texture. Wash any soiled eggs in water 43–46°C (110–115°F) in temperature, and to which a sanitizing agent has been added.

Store the eggs for incubating in a cool, moist place at a temperature of 10–15°C (50–59°F); they should be placed in egg trays, preferably on their sides rather than upended, and turned daily until such time as there are sufficient to hatch. Eggs can be kept in such a way for about ten days if they are to be set under a broody, and about a week if intended for the incubator.

Storage and optimum incubating conditions are best achieved by having specific housing and facilities at your disposal.

THE INCUBATION OF WATERFOWL EGGS

Domestic waterfowl eggs may be incubated naturally or artificially. If space permits and it is possible to hatch eggs under a broody hen or bantam, then it would be strongly advisable to do so. The hen is naturally more experienced at the job than even the most knowledgeable of incubator users, and there are no problems concerning temperatures, humidity, egg-turning and all the other potential difficulties that may beset those attempting to hatch artificially for the first time. Having said that, incubators undoubtedly have their place in the backyard, but it is strongly recommended that the novice poultry breeder arms themselves with a copy of *The New Incubation Book* by Dr A.F. Anderson Brown and G.E.S. Robbins (Hancock House Publishers, 2002).

The Broody Hen

It is important to choose the broody hen with great care. Although some of the lighter breeds will go broody, they are less inclined to remain so for the required period of time, and it is far better to use one of the heavier breeds or even a cross-bred hen (these, it must be said, quite often make the best broodies and foster mothers).

The best place to keep a broody hen whilst she is sitting is in a coop and run situated in a quiet corner well away from distractions and disturbance. Alternatively, it might be possible to sit her on her own nest in the corner of a larger shed or outbuilding until the chicks are hatched. Whatever method is chosen, the box should be the same dimensions as an ordinary nest box. An upturned grass sod or some fine damp earth should be included at the base of the box, as this will help form a 'saucer' for the nest and also provide much-needed humidity. On top of the soil, build up a nest of hay or straw (hay for preference) and be sure to pack it tightly into the corners so that no eggs can roll out. Dust the nest with flea powder. Make sure that the broody is ready to sit by first introducing her to a nest of 'dummy' eggs for twenty-four hours.

Do not overface the hen by giving her too many eggs to cover: if you do, there is a very real danger that some may become chilled because as she attempts to turn them, they will be pushed away from the perfect temperature, found directly under the breast of the bird, the place known as the 'brood spot'. It should be possible to accommodate four or five goose eggs under a large hen, but the actual number does of course depend on the size of the eggs and the size of the hen.

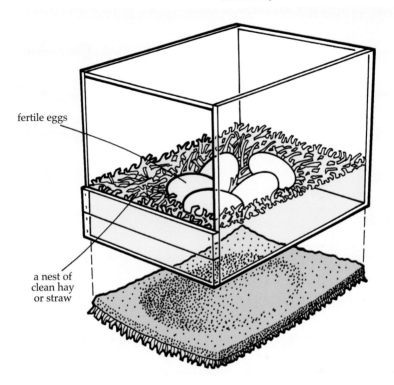

fertile eggs

a nest of
clean hay
or straw

An upturned grass sod or some fine damp earth should be included at the base of the nest box as this will help form a 'saucer' and will also provide much needed humidity. On top of the soil, build up a nest of hay or straw, and be sure to pack it tightly into the corners so that no eggs can roll out.

The hen should be allowed off the nest, or lifted off the eggs once a day for food, water and the opportunity to evacuate her bowels (any faeces in the nest must be immediately removed to prevent the eggs becoming soiled). A broody will use her beak and feet to regularly turn any 'normal'-sized eggs placed under her, but if she is required to sit on goose eggs, they should be turned by hand when she is off the nest. For the first week, ten minutes a day is all that she should be allowed, but after that the time can be increased up to about twenty minutes. Waterfowl eggs might need a little more moisture than other types of poultry and so it may pay to spray the eggs with aired water during the last week of incubation. ('Aired' water is water with the chill taken off it. This is best achieved by adding a little hot water to a volume of cold.)

Incubators are a useful asset, but be sure that you fully understand the manufacturer's operating instructions.

Artificial Incubation

Successful artificial incubation depends on a number of factors, some of the most important and obvious of which are a reliable heat source, humidity, air flow (ventilation) and regular egg-turning. Ducks and geese require very different incubator conditions to those of other poultry types – for a start, although humidity is very important to whatever is being hatched, it is particularly essential for domestic waterfowl because to control the normal weight loss of the egg that happens naturally during incubation, the correct humidity will prevent egg-shell membranes becoming too dry for hatching (it is also important to note that different humidity levels need to be provided at certain stages of incubation, with a very high humidity at the time of hatching). In natural situations, all these requirements would, of course, be provided by the broody duck or hen; in an artificial environment, they must be provided by the incubator.

Choosing an Incubator
If you wish to control the timing of your hatch, or cannot source a ready supply of broody hens when they are needed, there is no

alternative but to use an incubator. These come in various shapes and sizes, and each will have specific hatching instructions as recommended by the manufacturer – if you've bought a machine second-hand and there are no instructions, seek out someone who has a similar machine. Better still, there is almost always a manufacturer's address and phone number attached to any machine, so contact them and see if they would mind sending you a copy of instructions. Some of the smaller or older types might require the eggs to be turned twice daily by hand, but others are equipped with an egg-turning or tilt mechanism on a timer. There are two main types of incubator: the still air variety that relies on convection for ventilation, and forced air models, which tend to be larger and more expensive – with, correspondingly, more to adjust or go wrong!

Incubator Essentials
Make sure that the incubator is kept in a suitable shed or outbuilding – that is, one that retains a constant temperature. Modern electric units are nowadays so compact that it is tempting to situate them in the spare bedroom or study, but central heating and a stale

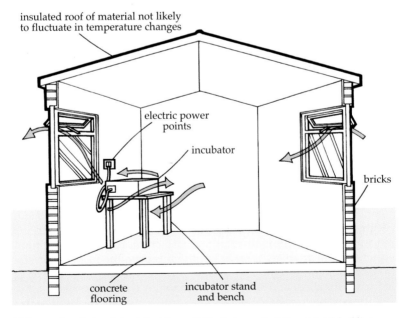

insulated roof of material not likely to fluctuate in temperature changes

electric power points

incubator

bricks

concrete flooring

incubator stand and bench

Make sure that the incubator is kept in a suitable shed or outbuilding. A brick building should have good insulation, a steady temperature, adequate ventilation and a concrete floor.

airflow will affect the results. A brick building with good insulation is likely to produce a better hatch than a draughty wooden shed or, worse still, a tin one, where the temperature fluctuates dramatically every time the sun shines. The ideal temperature is around 16–21°C (60–70°F). If the temperature drop is too great, it is quite likely that the incubator will be unable to maintain a steady temperature. It is therefore best to avoid incubating eggs during the coldest months if temperature regulation is likely to be a problem.

Adequate ventilation is also important, and if a room feels at all stuffy it could be affecting the eggs. A concrete floor is a good idea – not only is it easier to clean and disinfect, but also, as hatching time approaches, it can, if necessary, be kept damp so as to improve humidity in the incubator. Place the incubator on a level surface in a position that is not prone to vast fluctuations in temperature and humidity, and stand it on bricks or two pieces of solid square timber so that an adequate passage of air circulates around and *under* the incubator. Set up the incubator and bring it to temperature at least forty-eight hours before eggs are introduced, to enable the correct temperature and humidity to be established and to check that the thermostat is functioning normally.

Heat and Temperature
In most incubators, the thermometer should be positioned just above the top of the eggs. Manufacturers' recommended temperature settings could therefore lie anywhere between 38°C and 39.5°C (100.5°F and 103°F); in normal incubator operation, temperatures may fluctuate slightly, but they should not be allowed to pass outside this range. As the eggs develop, the embryos will give off some heat and this may require you to alter the thermostat setting slightly in order to decrease the temperature. Manufacturers often recommend the additional use of wet- and dry-bulb thermometers, which also measure humidity, but such readings are often inaccurate and an extra cause of worry.

Humidity
A suitable humidity must be maintained to prevent the eggs drying out too quickly. All incubators have one or more water containers, either trays or troughs, which should be kept topped up with water in order to maintain the appropriate humidity according to the type of incubator chosen. Always use aired water when it is necessary to refill them, and in hard water areas use boiled or distilled water. Relatively accurate electronic instruments for measuring humidity (called hygrometers) are now available, but the most useful of these

Candling

Duck and geese eggs are, because of their density, far more difficult to 'candle' than those of chickens or bantams. However, it is a useful operation to identify fertile and infertile eggs, any hairline cracks, and whether or not the humidity is correct at various stages of incubation. Candling machines are available commercially, but it is a simple matter to construct one's own: all you do is screw a light holder to the base of a wooden box, and cut a hole, roughly egg-shaped in size, out of the top. By switching the light on and holding the egg over the hole, it is a simple matter to see whether or not the egg is fertile and at the correct stage of development. To do this you do, of course, need to have an accepted guideline of development, the best of which can be found in *The New Incubation Book* by Dr A.F. Anderson Brown and G.E.S. Robbins (Blaine, WA: Hancock House Publishers, 2002).

are quite expensive and in the hands of an inexperienced person are a bane, rather than a boon. It is far better to check humidity by assessing the effects on the egg, rather than obtaining actual measurements; this can be done in the operation known as 'candling' (*see* panel).

Ventilation
Ventilation is necessary to ensure a good supply of oxygen and, most importantly, to remove the carbon dioxide produced, in order that it does not poison the developing chicks. Ventilation will also affect both the humidity and the temperature, and so great care must be taken to set the ventilation control according to the manufacturer's instructions. On some incubators, a flap covering ventilation holes may need to be moved; in others, the number of holes that are left open may need to be altered. Frequent checks should be made to ensure that nothing is preventing adequate ventilation. If using an incubator with an insulated quilt cover that fits over the observation dome, ensure that the quilt does not block the top ventilation hole.

Turning
In natural circumstances, a female duck or goose brooding her own eggs will turn them several times daily with her feet and may even

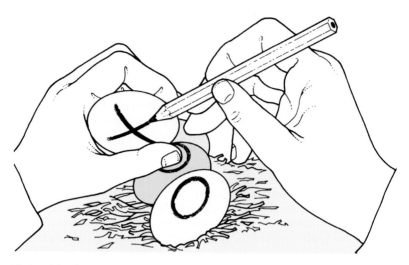

Mark each hatching egg lightly with an 'X' drawn in pencil on one side and an 'O' on the opposite side.

be seen pushing and moving them with her bill. In the incubator, there is no such natural help and so it is all down to either the mechanics of the machine itself, or the dexterous hands of the operator to do artificially what the sitting parent does naturally. Turning the eggs needs to be carried out at least twice a day, and in the days when I used a Glevum incubator, it was necessary to turn each one by hand. To make sure I'd not missed one, before setting, I would mark each egg lightly with an 'X' drawn in pencil on one side and an 'O' on the opposite side – in that way, all eggs should have been showing an 'O' after turning each evening, and 'X' after the morning's attention. Such an operation is slightly time-consuming and obviously requires a twice daily opening of the incubator and with it the risk of altering temperature and humidity. In these modern times, an automatic egg-turning facility for the incubator is a very high priority, and many new machines come thus equipped.

BROODING DUCKLINGS AND GOSLINGS

Goslings and ducklings can be successfully brooded by broody chicken hens. Always start with clean quarters: any small building, garage or corner can be used as a brooding area provided that it is warm, draught-proof and rodent free – there is nothing that rats like better than ducklings and goslings. By far the best place to house your hen and her offspring is in a traditional coop and run, which can be moved periodically on to fresh grass.

If she has not hatched them herself, a broody hen can be encouraged to accept youngsters by introducing them in the following way. Let her sit on a nest of dummy or infertile eggs for a week, and then on the evening when the chicks arrive, take one and place it under her breast feathers. If she takes to this one, wait an hour or so before introducing the others. Before introducing any chicks, be certain that the broody bird is free of lice and mites, but be careful that any preparations used are not likely to be harmful to her newly introduced brood.

The hen will need grain and the youngsters will need the protein supplied by good quality chick crumbs or perhaps one of the alternatives mentioned in the previous chapter. Both will need plenty of fresh, clean water supplied in a container that will not allow the

Clean water should be given in the types of drinker that preclude young birds from getting wet or, worse still, falling in and drowning.

young to get wet or, worse still, fall in and drown. And yes, despite the fact that ducks and geese are aquatic birds, ducklings and goslings are nevertheless very susceptible to chilling or drowning until such time as they begin to grow protective feathers.

Brooding by Artificial Means

Artificial hatching generally necessitates artificial brooding – although, as can be seen in the previous section, it may be possible to introduce incubator-hatched birds to a broody hen. There are many varieties of artificial brooder on the market. In some, heated wiring traverses the upper part of the chamber, some centimetres above the chicks; in others a warm iron plate radiates heat in the same way, or warmed air is brought in by a system of flues and openings. The simplest arrangement is basically a box over which a heat supply is hung. For very small numbers of birds all you need is a large cardboard box, some shavings, a heat lamp, a feeder and water. The brooding area should be dry, reasonably well lit and ventilated, and free from draughts. Cover the floor with a few centimetres of absorbent litter material such as wood shavings, under which you should place a layer of paper sacks or newspaper.

A special building is not required to house the brooder, but it must provide protection from the weather and be reasonably well lit and ventilated. For brooding small numbers, any small building may be used. For brooding larger numbers, a barn or poultry house is recommended. The brooder must, however, be sited away from draughts. Ducklings suffer from cramp if kept on a cold surface, and ideally they should be reared off the floor, on a wooden surface. Dampness is likely to be more of a problem with ducklings and goslings than it is when brooding other types of poultry, and so good management will require the removal of wet spots and the addition of clean, dry litter on a regular basis.

Heat Source
When rearing under artificial brooders, remember that young waterfowl do not need as high a temperature as other forms of domestic fowl, and a heat pattern of around 30°C (86°F) is ideal for the first few days; gradually reduce the temperature over the course of three to four weeks. Experiment with the height of the lamp above the brooder to obtain the correct temperature before adding the chicks, and once they are installed, watch their behaviour and adjust the height of the lamp if necessary. Avoid using an infra-red bulb for ducklings and goslings – being messy in their drinking

The simplest brooder arrangement is basically a box over which a heat source is hung.

habits, there is a good chance that they will cause the lamps to blow by splashing water on them. It is far better to use the dull emitters, as they are more robust and will not shatter. Allow one 250-watt dull emitter per twenty-five goslings or thirty ducklings.

Obviously having the heat source set at the right height and temperature is important, but in many instances, the behaviour of the young birds is often a better guide than a thermometer, and much can be learned by watching them closely for the first couple of hours. When the brooder temperature is too hot, the birds will crowd away from the heat, and when it is uncomfortably cold, they will tend to huddle together under the brooder or crowd in corners: there should be a central spot that is too hot, with a ring of comfortable birds around it. If you watch an individual bird from this ring, you will notice that every so often it will get up, have a run around, try out the food and water, and then return for a quick warm-up. At night, the birds should form a circle around the brooder.

An easily cleanable brooding arrangement, generally suitable for young ducks and geese, but in this case used specifically for the rearing of ornamental waterfowl.

'Hardening Off'

Like plants in a greenhouse, young ducks and geese need hardening off. Reared by a broody hen, they will do this naturally, but artificially reared birds should, as we have seen, have their heat source reduced over a period of three to four weeks. In good weather it may be possible to turn off the heat completely during the day from three weeks, but it should normally be reconnected for the nighttime for about another week. By this time both naturally and artificially reared birds should have access to an outside run in which, depending on the weather, they will spend most of their day, only returning to 'mum' for a quick warm-up.

At three weeks, ducklings and goslings should already have started growing proper feathers on their backs, and as the wing feathers develop more quickly than the rest, they are already gaining some protection against the elements. By the age of about six weeks they are fully feathered (but not with adult plumage) and can be removed from the broody or heater.

— 6 —

Health and Hygiene

Geese really are the least troublesome of all domestic fowl as far as health and hygiene are concerned. Ducks require a little more care and attention, but even so, provided that they have access to fresh ground, water deep enough to wash their heads in, their houses are regularly cleaned and disinfected and they are not kept in over-crowded conditions, they are unlikely to suffer from any of the health problems that occasionally affect commercial flocks of domestic duck.

Domestic waterfowl are nothing like as prone to ectoparasites as poultry, but nevertheless keep an eye out for mites, lice and fleas. Whilst not life-threatening, they will certainly affect the bird's appearance, behaviour and general well-being. Parasitic fungi can also attack the respiratory system, with mouldy straw and damp grain being a frequent source of such infections, so cleanliness is of paramount importance.

All types of poultry have their own characteristic smells. You should house your ducks and geese in such a way that the odour is not offensive to either you or your next-door neighbours – this can all be done by providing adequate ventilation in the poultry house, not overstocking, and establishing a regular weekly (or more often, if necessary) cleaning routine.

A REGULAR ROUTINE

Issues of hygiene are mostly a matter of common sense – if the night-time housing of ducks and geese is clean, light and well ven-tilated, and the floor well drained and covered with litter that is reg-ularly changed, there should be few or no hygiene problems. Inevitably, dark corners and the backs of nesting boxes will encour-age mites and fleas to take up residence, and so must all be routine-ly soaked with a dilution of disinfectant such as 'Poultry Shield'. This will clear away the red mite themselves as well as their eggs,

Issues of hygiene are mostly a matter of common sense – regular cleaning and a supply of clean, parasite-free litter and/or nest-box material will all help in ensuring that your birds keep healthy.

and is, according to David Bland of SPR, West Sussex, '...the only solution that can penetrate the waxy egg coatings. Poultry Shield has no harmful effect on the birds, even if inadvertently splashed on their food. Keep the house well dusted on a weekly basis with "Diatom", which, being a natural product, has no ill effect on the birds and, if consumed by them, will help reduce any internal build-up of worms. Diatom not only keeps red mite at bay, but all other types of lice and mites'.

Wheat straw or wood shavings are the traditional litter for a nest box, and there can be no doubt that collecting an egg from such a place is a pleasurable exercise. It is not, however, the cleanest or most hygienic bedding: straw, unless it was perfectly cut and dried and meticulously stored, is potentially subject to fungal diseases such as aspergillosis, especially once soiled by a few ducks and geese tramping in mud and damp, and is the ideal home for para-sites. If you do have to use straw, use only wheat and certainly not barley, which has its own problems due to the 'ears' and husks. Personally I prefer to use shredded paper, which is available in bales from most agricultural suppliers. It absorbs the dirt and damp and does not provide a ready home to unwanted guests – the only disadvantage being that, in a sudden gust of wind your chicken run might look as if there's been an American-style ticker-tape parade in the vicinity!

Feeding and watering locations are important areas to consider, and it goes without saying that drinkers and feeders must be moved periodically in order to prevent a build-up of problems. No matter what the type of poultry being kept, the bird's ability to fight off an initial disease challenge is most important, as this will help them avoid becoming prone to secondary infections – sick birds have a reduced feed intake and therefore consume fewer initial nutrients.

Nutritionally, feed the correct ration for the stage of growth of the bird. An excess of some nutrients can be as harmful as a deficiency in some birds, and a digestive upset leading to diarrhoea results in wet litter, which encourages a spread of disease. Never forget that an all-important daily component of the bird's diet is fresh water, and a suspicious water supply is frequently associated with the spread of all manner of infections.

If you ever have to go away, and doing so means that you will need to call upon the services of a family member or neighbour to look after the birds in your absence, it will pay to explain carefully as much as you can regarding the daily and weekly routine. As well as explaining verbally, it does no harm at all to leave a typed list of jobs to be done pinned somewhere in the feed shed. Make sure that the list contains the telephone number of a fellow fancier some-where in the area – it is far easier for anyone concerned about a par-ticular problem to phone and ask someone to come and give their opinion and help within an hour or two, than it is for the neighbour to ring you.

The list should also contain the vet's telephone number, and if you are particularly efficient, you could ring your vet before you go away in order to inform them that 'Fred Bloggs' will be looking after your birds for the next two weeks – this should make explanations easier in the unhappy event that 'Fred' has to call the surgery when you are away. It is, of course, imperative that you ask your fellow poultry keeper's permission to leave their telephone number on your list.

It is not uncommon for those looking after their friend's birds to overfeed; this may mean that the adequate amount of food you have carefully worked out that your birds will require during your absence is finished before your return. To avoid the problem of a possible food shortage, arrange with your supplier that, in case of emergency, they will supply your friend directly, and allow you to settle any amount owing on your return.

SOME POSSIBLE PROBLEMS

Even though there should be very few problems as long as ducks and geese are correctly kept, it would be foolish to ignore the fact that sometimes troubles do occur; it is therefore just as well to be able to recognize them, and then to know how to treat them, and even better, how to avoid them in the first place. Most, it must be admitted, are only likely to surface where larger numbers of ducks and geese are being bred and reared commercially; as a small-scale rearer and keeper of waterfowl, you are very unlikely to have experience of them, so don't worry unnecessarily.

Avian Influenza

Although there is much recent media attention concerning avian influenza or 'bird flu', the disease has actually been recognized since 1878; by 1901 its cause had been identified as a virus and it was given the name of 'fowl plague'. In 1955, its relationship to the mammalian influenza A viruses had been proven, but it was not until the 1970s that it was realized that vast pools of influenza A

Try and keep all feeders and drinkers as clean as the day they were purchased.

viruses also exist in the feral bird population. It is this latter fact that makes the control of any serious outbreak more difficult to put into effect, especially where poultry are kept outdoors. The avian influenza virus, known as H5N1, breeds in the respiratory and intestinal tracts of infected birds and is transmitted from bird to bird, either by coughing and sneezing or through the faeces. The clinical signs are a difficulty in breathing, or simply sudden death.

Routine bio-security precautions to prevent the spread of bird flu include keeping visitors away from your birds, ensuring that all feeding and drinking utensils are kept clean and made inaccessible to wild bird stocks, and adding a product such as 'Vanodine' to the water every day. Occasionally spraying the insides of the night-time quarters with a virucide will also help. If you have any suspicions that your birds might be showing signs of bird flu, you must notify your vet and/or the appropriate government authority straight-away. Please note that it is the high pathogenic strain of AIV that is referred to here; the low pathogenic strain would not be recognized in flocks because there are few, if any, disease indications. Such infections pass in and out of a flock within fourteen days, and can be compared to minor common colds in humans, although they are *not* related.

Duck Plague, *aka* Duck Virus Enteritis

Duck virus enteritis is caused by a herpes virus and is most likely to be noticed during late spring or early summer. It can affect all ages, ranging from week-old ducklings right through to mature birds, and depending on the age, may show itself in many ways. The first signs are often a loss of appetite, ruffled feathers, soiled vents, watery diarrhoea and some nasal discharge. Affected birds might struggle to keep their balance, often attempting to use their wings for support. In ducklings, symptoms can also include dehydration, loss of weight, a blue coloration of the beaks, and bloodstained vents. In laying stock there is also likely to be a significant drop in egg production, though this is not always the case. If you suspect birds of succumbing to this disease, contact your veterinary surgeon immediately, as they may be able to provide a live virus vaccine.

Were you ever to hear of a fellow duck keeper whose flock has been affected by the virus, it might pay, once the disease has past, to try and buy one of their remaining drakes for your flock so as to pass on their natural immunity against the disease. This type of immunity is claimed to be far superior to simple vaccination, and if you keep ornamental ducks and geese, it is more efficient.

Duck Septicaemia, *aka* Anatipestifer Infection

Although it is necessary to be aware of potential problems, there is a very real danger of thinking the worst. For example, one of the symptoms of anatipestifer infection (duck septicaemia) is watery eyes – but in all probability 'weepy' eyes are more likely to be caused by the conditions during a hot, dry summer. True anatipestifer infection is a bacterial infection affecting ducklings most commonly between the ages of four and nine weeks old. Symptoms do indeed include watery eyes, but also ruffled feathers, green diarrhoea, a staggering gait and an inability to stand. Severely affected birds sit with their heads tucked close to their body, or continually shake their head. It is possible to protect by vaccination.

Worms

Parasitic worms are generally referred to as helminths – hence the treatments for worms are termed anthelmintics. Some helminths can live inside a host and cause no harm; others, however, can lead to serious problems. The secret in dealing with them is to break the cycle by which the birds become infected, and this is best done by a regular programme of worming – it is a safe bet that geese and ducks will be reinfested unless a periodic worming routine is maintained. To further minimize or to prevent reinfestation, you should also periodically rotate runs, separate ducks of different age groups, and never overstock.

Ducks can be affected by the same worms that affect all other poultry types. All ages are affected, but older ducks have better resistance to worms than ducklings and generally show milder effects. Young ducklings are particularly susceptible, and heavy worm infestations may kill them or stunt their growth. Indications as to the presence of any worms can vary, but generally symptoms include a loss of weight, even though the amount of food being consumed is maintained, diarrhoea (that can range from frothy yellow to blood-tinged) and an unusual lethargy. Birds heavily infested with roundworms or hairworms may die suddenly, though more commonly they become weak and die after a period of time. Good pen management and regular worming will, however, go a long way towards ensuring that worms never become a serious problem.

Roundworms
Roundworms are, as their name suggests, round and smooth, whereas the tapeworm is segmented. The female roundworm lays

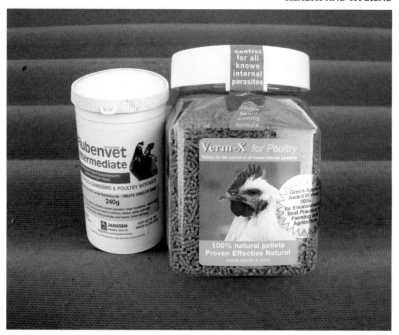

To avoid problems, adopt into your management programme a regular worming routine, using a medically approved wormer such as 'Flubenvet'.

her eggs in the intestines of domesticated fowl; they are eventually excreted and are then picked up by other birds, hatching in the intestine of the new host; and the whole cycle begins again.

Tapeworms
Tapeworm eggs may also pass through the bird via its faeces, or be retained in one of the segmented sections of the worm. These sections periodically break off and are also excreted, at which point they are sometimes eaten by small invertebrates that become the temporary host. If a duck then eats that host, the cycle continues, but unlike the roundworm, if only the eggs or segmented sections are ingested by the bird, they will not develop into more tapeworms.

Hairworms
Probably the least known of all worm infections, the hairworm can, nevertheless, cause problems. Unlike other worms they are not so easy to see, and tend to be found in the 'blind gut' (caeca) of the bird.

Gizzard Worms
Gizzard worms work their way under the gizzard lining, and will, if unrecognized and therefore untreated, cause both ducks and geese quickly to become sick and die. They are reddish in colour.

How to Avoid Worm Infestation
To avoid such problems, include in your management programme at least an annual worming routine using a medically approved wormer such as 'Flubenvet', produced by Jansson. There are in fact two choices of worm treatment available to the poultry keeper: broad spectrum chemicals effective against the major groups of worms, and narrow-spectrum products that are effective against a particular type of worm. Ask your vet or agricultural supplier to suggest the most suitable form of worming treatment. Legally it is not permissible to treat birds with a medication that has not been expressly developed for the purpose, but there are alternatives that can be legitimately prescribed by a veterinary surgeon.

It should be noted that if ducks and geese have volumes of water in which to swim and bathe, they are capable of flushing out these parasites faster than they can reproduce, and it is only when they are kept in small runs and only have access to stagnant water that the main problems occur. If there is no pond available, deep bucket drinkers in which the water is changed each day will be of great benefit. Even so, worm on at least an annual basis.

Salmonellosis

The symptoms most often found in waterfowl suffering from salmonellosis are, typically, a refusal to eat, general dejection, diarrhoea, and a tendency to fall forwards when attempting to walk or stand. It can lead to high mortality in ducklings, so it is important to practise good husbandry. Several types of salmonella organisms are found in dirty litter, which is another good reason why all duck and geese shelters should be regularly cleaned and disinfected. The organisms also have the potential to infect a bird's liver, spleen, heart, ovary and reproductive tract. These organisms can also cause food poisoning in humans by being transferred through eggs that have been laid in dirty conditions.

In the days when ducks were kept on farm ponds into which all the slurry and effluent found its way, the disease also used to find its way into the ducks in the course of their mating with drakes on the pond. Again, clean water is extremely important in helping to prevent such diseases. As the normal domestic goose prefers to mate on dry land, there is less chance of geese becoming infected by salmonellae in the same way.

Accidental Poisoning

Geese and ducks are fiercely inquisitive – if there's an open bag to explore, a bucket left within their reach, or an interesting puddle of liquid in which to dabble their beaks, they will. It is therefore not surprising that fatalities occur due to carelessness on the part of their owners. When birds are allowed access to the garden, for example, make sure that there are no slug pellets lying around as these are fatal to ducklings and goslings. Salt, too, is a potential killer, and it only requires the consumption of small quantities to bring on diarrhoea, weakness, partial paralysis and intermittent muscular spasms. Antifreeze solutions (ethylene glycol) are attractive to all forms of livestock as they are sweet and sugary to the taste – ducks and geese are no exception, and any solutions left around will be consumed with pleasure; taken in sufficient quantities, they could result in muscle weakness and death. If, as is the case on many smallholdings, ducks and geese have free range in and around outbuildings, make sure that any insecticides and medications are stored well out of reach of inquisitive bills – it is surprising just how far the neck of a goose can stretch.

Accidental poisoning can also occur when birds are given, or have access to, food that has been incorrectly stored (perhaps in warm, humid conditions) and has gone mouldy. The symptoms can include lack of appetite, general lethargy and liver and kidney failure, leading to death. Often, dead birds will be found lying with their legs stretched out to the rear, although obviously this cannot be taken as a definite diagnosis of this particular problem.

Normally ducks discriminate against most poisonous plants, provided they are not kept underfed or overstocked. The accidental ingestion of the occasional poisonous seed and leaf does not usually produce any adverse reactions, and it is only when the poisonous plant becomes a substantial part of the diet, or when minute quantities are consumed regularly over a long time, that signs become evident. Yew berries are known to be poisonous to humans, and yet they are not to the wild birds that regularly eat them in season. It is presumed that the reason they can do so is that it is only the seeds that are toxic, and these pass untouched through the bird.

The amount of plant material that will produce signs of poisoning depends to a large degree on the nature of its toxicity, the part of the plant ingested, and its stage of growth. Some naturally occurring

Accidental poisoning can occur as a result of ducks and geese gaining access to the most unlikely sources, including salt, anti-freeze, slug pellets, plants and mouldy food.

poisons are only present in the plant seasonally; for example, there have been recent cases in France where sportsmen have shot and eaten wild quail and become ill from doing so, and yet at other times have not suffered any ill effects whatsoever. It is thought this is because the quail eat a seed from a member of the mint family, which is only poisonous at certain times of the year.

Feather Pecking

Only on rare occasions is feather pecking seen amongst ducks and geese; in other forms of poultry it is far more common a problem. However, feather pecking or quill pulling can become a habit in larger flocks of ducks, and is usually caused by crowding too many birds into too small an area. The remedy for this problem is to de-beak the ducks in much the same manner as chickens, as also if cannibalism occurs. However, other preventative measures need to be considered first, as this behaviour is most likely to be the result of insanitary surroundings or inherent weakness due to breeding, and is a sure sign that management is faulty. By far the best solution is to reduce flock size and provide a larger area in which birds can roam.

Sunstroke

Believe it or not, young ducklings and goslings are susceptible to sunstroke, which can prove fatal. Also, it is useful to know that ducklings are less able to tolerate the sun immediately after eating. Symptoms include extreme lethargy, very high temperatures, a staggering gait, and possibly convulsions. It is therefore important that all pens containing young birds should have adequate shade: if natural shade is not available, provide some type of shelter. Cold water can be fatal to overheated ducklings. Therefore, leave water for ducklings in a warm place until the chill has gone off it before pouring it into their drinking vessels.

Staggers

On the subject of water, there is a condition known amongst poultry fanciers as 'staggers', which is commonly caused by a temporary

Some crested ducks are troubled with intracranial body fat, which, depending on the size and location, may lead to varying degrees of immobility. On occasions, their crests have also been known to harbour parasites and, during periods of extreme cold, suffer from frost. Because of these potential problems, they are not recommended as beginner's birds.

103

shortage of drinking water. If the birds feed before the water is replenished, death usually follows in a short time.

Angel Wing

Although it is not a disease or a problem – unless you intend to show or otherwise exhibit your birds – there is a condition of ducks and geese known amongst fanciers as 'angel wing', where the last joint of the wing is twisted and the wing feathers point outwards. It is more common in geese, and typically in either the left wing or both wings, only rarely in the right wing alone. For some unknown reason, ganders seem to develop it more than females. Its cause is thought to be nutritional, possibly due to the ingestion of unlimited, high protein, high energy feed when the birds are adolescent, as a result of which they grow unnaturally fast and their wing feathers apparently outgrow the strength of the wing to support them.

There is a condition of ducks and geese known amongst fanciers as 'angel wing', which is where the last joint of the wing is twisted and the wing feathers point out. It is more common in geese, typically in either the left wing or both wings; it is rarely seen in the right wing only.

VITAMINS; BIOTICS AND PRO-NUTRIENTS

There are a number of nutrients that aid general health and assist in immune responses against the likelihood of disease and sickness. Vitamin A is important for the development, quality and repair of epithelial tissues that line the digestive tract, secretory glands and the entire surface of the skin. A diseased gut has an impaired ability to absorb vitamin A. Vitamin E is an efficient biological antioxidant that prevents tissue damage and maintains cellular structure and metabolism. It also has a role to play in enhancing immunity. Selenium is a trace element that protects the active cells of the immune system and helps fight off any disease challenges. Its role in nutrition and reproduction cannot be overplayed, and significantly improved bio-availability of this vital trace element from an organic source such as 'Sel-Plex' will result in enhanced fertility, hatchability and chick viability. Zinc is another important trace element necessary in assisting any source of vitamin A into the bird's metabolism.

Probiotics are viable micro-organisms added to the diet to improve the gut's microbial balance, and prebiotics are non-digestible feed additives that beneficially affect the bird by selectively stimulating the growth of beneficial micro-organisms; herbs, spices and botanical extracts can be included under the term 'pro-nutrients'. These have been shown to help the bird overcome physiological and environmental stresses, and also to reduce the effects of disease challenges such as coccidiosis.

Birds suffering from a loss of appetite for one reason or another tend to look huddled and depressed. To overcome this problem you need to have complete control over drinking water for a seven-day period so you can add to it a multi-vitamin such as 'Stressless'. This particular product has been specifically designed and patented by a highly qualified veterinary surgeon, has been tested commercially, and is now available to the small-scale poultry keeper.

KILLING BIRDS

From time to time it may be necessary to kill a sick bird (or even, of course, one for the table). This can be carried out quickly and humanely by taking the bird's legs in your left hand and taking up its head in your right, with your fingers under the bill. Bend the head back, and with a positive downward thrust, dislocate the head from the neck (be aware of the fact that young ducks have very tender skin and, without care, their heads will come off very easily).

The same principles do not apply to the dispatching of geese owing to their weight and length. It is the opinion of most poultry keepers that the quickest and most humane method is to take the bird by the legs, lay its head on the ground ('chin' on ground, beak facing forwards) so that you are looking at its back, place a broom handle over the neck and, holding it firmly in place with your feet (one either side of the bird), pull upwards on the legs with both hands; this dislocates the neck in the same way as for the ducks.

Before attempting to cull any birds for the first time, every effort should be made to seek the advice and training of an experienced operator.

A Ten-Point Plan for Health and Hygiene

1. Make a point of leaning on the gate and watching stock – birds should be feeding, drinking, and obviously happy. Identify and deal immediately with any that are not.
2. Trust your instincts and worry if you notice that all is not well, even if there are no obvious symptoms and you have nothing more to go on than the look in a bird's eye or a hint of depression – when trying to determine a possible problem it always pays to think 'cause and effect'.
3. Make a friend of your vet and local fellow poultry fanciers – they might identify problems more quickly than you, saving much time and heartache.
4. Clean housing and equipment regularly. Thoroughly disinfect broody coops, incubators and brooders after each intake.
5. Where possible, move your stock on to fresh ground every few months, or at the very least, arrange two pens side by side so that one is periodically rested.
6. Be careful where you go – any place where poultry is found could be the source of potential health problems, and that includes any poultry-keeping neighbours, shows and auctions. A disinfectant footbath at home is not a bad idea, but it is only effective if replenished on a daily basis.
7. Isolate any newly purchased stock from others for a period of seven to fourteen days. Do the same with your own birds after a show, just in case they have contracted some ailment from other poultry at the show. Whilst this is very unlikely, it is nevertheless a sensible precaution.

8. Carry out a regular regime of dusting or spraying your birds in order to counteract lice and fleas. How often this should be done depends on the product being used.

9. Feed a proper balanced diet – while 'old-timers' would habitually feed a hot mash, such a preparation quickly becomes sour and stale. Ensuring that feeds supply nutrients to optimize growth and health all helps towards ensuring that any disease challenges can be successfully overcome. Feed only twice a day, and pick up all feeders after a period of 10–15 minutes.

10. Vermin such as rats and mice can cause health problems amongst any poultry types, therefore it is important to maintain a careful poison-baiting programme, and to keep feed stores and penning sheds clear of old bags and rubbish – all of which encourage rats and mice to take up residence.

Preening is the bird's way of ridding itself of parasites, and also of distributing natural waterproofing oils throughout the feathers.

— 7 —

Showing and Exhibiting

Although not quite as popular a pastime as the showing and exhibiting of chickens and bantams, ducks and geese do have their own classes and categories in many poultry shows, as well as regional and national events devoted entirely to domestic waterfowl. The majority of the biggest waterfowl shows are usually held in the three months before Christmas when birds are at their best after the autumn moult and a summer spent in 'eclipse'.

The British Waterfowl Association is the only UK organization to cater for both wildfowl and domestic waterfowl. Within the BWA, there are specialist committees, one of which is that devoted to the exhibiting of ducks and geese. The Domestic Waterfowl and Showing Committee is involved in running the BWA annual national show, whilst the Membership, Education and Publicity Committee organize other displays at national events such as the Royal Show and the Game Fair. It is interesting to note that although wildfowl are no longer exhibited at shows, they are occasionally seen for sale at certain venues.

SHOW SCHEDULES, STANDARDS AND JUDGES

As with every type of showing, no matter whether it is cattle or flowers, there are certain standards to which your chosen breed of duck must conform. Breed standards can be found in the book *British Poultry Standards*, the poultryman's 'bible', and your birds should be as near as possible to those laid out within its pages. Many of the aspects to be judged will be the same no matter what the breed, but the points awarded will vary somewhat. For example, at the time of writing, the carriage and stance of an Indian Runner is worth a maximum of twenty points, whereas the same for a Call duck or Rouen carries a maximum of only ten points. Likewise, the perfectly coloured Blue Swedish may be awarded as many as thirty points by the judges, but the Pekin can only ever hope to gain ten. Several well known and highly respected people in the world of exhibition waterfowl believe that the standards should be as uncomplicated as possible, not only for ease of use by judges, but also for the exhibitors themselves.

Judges for the relevant categories are often chosen from a judges' panel that features in the *Poultry Club's Year Book*, and they will have had to pass several exams in order to qualify in one of the four categories: panels A, B, C and D. In order to gain promotion up the ladder to the level of a grade 'A' judge, a total of seven examinations will have to be taken. One of the seven is the 'Waterfowl Test', which is organized in conjunction with the BWA. Candidates have the option of specializing by taking four separate tests – geese, heavy ducks, light ducks and bantam ducks – which when taken individually, will qualify a judge for panel C level and also BWA and Poultry Club shows. Some Europeans insist that their poultry judges attend regular 'refresher' courses in order to ensure that they are *au fait* with all that is going on in the show world, but as yet there are no such compulsory requirements in the UK.

It is necessary to have shown competence and to have gained various qualifications before being allowed to judge at any poultry show.

Understanding Show Schedules

It is obviously important to fully understand the show schedule, and also to check out any clauses specific to the particular club or society. 'Must have been the property of the exhibitor and been in their possession for at least two months', or 'Must have been bred by the exhibitor' may find their way into the small print, and the comments must be observed and adhered to.

As a general rule, schedules are available from the show secretary at least a month in advance of the intended date. It is all too easy to let the enclosed entry form sit on the mantelpiece or on the desk, fully intending to 'deal with it later', but from my experience, it is far better to fill it in and return it as soon as possible to avoid the risk of applying for entry after the given closing date – usually about ten to fourteen days before the show. Be sure that you understand fully the different categories and enter your birds in the right one – if you are in any doubt, ask the advice of an experienced fancier met through your local smallholding or poultry club. It also pays to visit several shows before entering your own stock, and you will learn far more of what is expected as a result.

This particular Hookbill sailed through all the relevant classes in the schedule and was eventually awarded 'Best of Breed'.

Look, Listen and Learn

The need for newcomers to spend time at some of the larger shows before entering their own birds cannot be overemphasized, and perhaps the best shows of all to go to in order to look, listen and learn are the annual British Waterfowl Association National Show, and the Devon and Cornwall, where examples of virtually all the breeds and types can be found. Of the two, I am told that the latter is the largest and has the greatest number of show entries – ranging between 700 and 1,000 – its popularity due apparently to the abnormally high level of interest in waterfowl in that particular area. This show and others like it are a 'must' for smallholders who are seeking a specific variety to keep, because not only can you see the type of bird that you might like to raise, but you can also talk to the breeders about the values and benefits of the breed in order to see if it will fit in with your own personal and possibly very demanding requirements.

In addition to the show 'proper', there is often a separate selling area with stewards on hand to inform potential buyers about the birds for sale, as well as a plethora of displays with all manner of

The need for newcomers to spend time at some of the larger shows before entering their own birds cannot be overemphasized.

waterfowl arks, nest boxes and pens on offer. Club stands are also very much in evidence, and they do much to promote their own particular breed and answer questions – don't worry that yours might sound ridiculous – rest assured, they have heard much sillier ones, and after all, everyone has to start somewhere. On occasions you might be lucky enough to find a judge's masterclass included, in which prominent waterfowl judges assess birds and give a description on each bird to other judges, thus enabling everyone to benefit from their experiences.

SELECTING BIRDS

Select your potential show birds and accustom them to an exhibition pen; although, unlike other types of poultry, ducks and geese do tend to stand well and in a typical show stance quite naturally, a little acclimatization and encouragement will never go amiss. If you have no access to a penning room and/or show pens, then at least spend some time handling your birds in the same way that

Show birds need to be confident in being handled.

Handling Ducks for the Show Pen

Approach the cage slowly, open the door quietly and prepare to remove the bird, head first. Manoeuvre the bird until it stands with its head to your right or left, and then reach into the pen and across the back of the bird with your right hand (or, if left-handed, with your left) before gently but firmly grasping the most distant wing at the shoulder. Keep the wing folded and close to the bird's body. Rotate the bird in the cage so that its head is pointing towards you and the open door. Slide your free hand, palm upwards, underneath the bird's breast. Simultaneously, grasp the duck's right leg (just above the hock joint) between your thumb and index finger while clasping the left leg between the second and third fingers; this places your index and second fingers between its legs. The keel bones should now be resting on the palm of your hand. Bring the bird out of the cage head first, keeping its head towards you. After holding the bird for a while, open the wings and examine various parts of the body. Always return the bird to the cage head first, and lower it gently to the floor of the cage.

a judge will be assumed to handle them at the show. Frightened birds tend to stand in a crouched, rather than normal position, thus their true type is not revealed to the judge. Birds unaccustomed to handling may also struggle when examined. Obviously geese, being rather large and heavy, are shown and handled differently to ducks, but nevertheless the basic principles remain the same.

Some General Pointers

It is important for any bird to be in good health and prime condition if it is to have any chance of winning – an underweight specimen will not possess the smooth form and overall appearance that will catch the judge's eye. Ducks in particular are prone to poor skin condition, and during the winter, dead skin can accumulate on their feet, legs and bill. These areas should be attended to well before the beginning of the show season, and experienced exhibitors often advocate the application of Vaseline or other natural moisturizers. It is also important to ensure that birds are free of parasites, including worms, mites and lice.

Damaged feathers will obviously ruin a bird's chances in the show pen, and any broken or soiled feathers must be removed in plenty of time for them to regrow. Provided that birds are kept in clean quarters for at least a week before the due date, and that they are provided with clean bathing daily, they should preen and oil their feathers into superb condition. Also, do not forget to trim the toenails if necessary, and be sure to cut them in plenty of time: if you leave it until the last minute to trim them and you nick a blood vessel in the nail, blood will stain the plumage. If the toenails do need trimming, use dog nail trimmers and then file them lightly with a nail file.

Light or white plumage that is heavily soiled may need to be washed, but this is more usual with exhibition chickens and bantams than it is with ducks and geese. Dark-coloured ducks such as the Rouen breed very seldom need to be washed unless their plumage has become severely soiled. Wash birds at least two or three days before the show in order that they can preen themselves back into pristine condition, and also imbibe their feathers with naturally secreted oils from the preening gland found at the base of the tail.

Crested birds need particular care when being prepared for the show bench.

After washing, place the birds in cages in a warmish room. If they have to be returned to their usual housing, it is important to use plenty of shavings as litter in order to keep them from becoming soiled again.

TRANSPORTING YOUR BIRDS

To transport your birds to the show or exhibition, some sort of sturdy container will be required. For many years I felt very much the poor relation when I arrived at the show with my birds in supermarket cardboard boxes, when all around me competitors were transporting theirs in purpose-made wicker baskets. Eventually a favourite aunt had one of these made for me at the local workshops for the blind, and I was able to carry my poultry with pride. In actual fact it doesn't really matter what carrying boxes are constructed

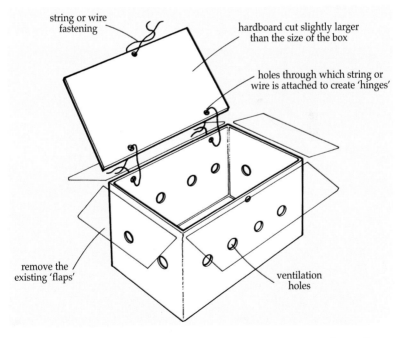

string or wire fastening

hardboard cut slightly larger than the size of the box

holes through which string or wire is attached to create 'hinges'

remove the existing 'flaps'

ventilation holes

Cardboard boxes used as carrying boxes take up no valuable storage space as they can be disposed of immediately after use. Make a box more secure by removing the flaps at the top and replacing them with a piece of hardboard cut fractionally oversize, and construct hinges and fasteners by threading wire or string through small holes pierced in the box and lid.

of, but they should be large enough to allow poultry to turn around and keep cool. Large boxes will help prevent feather damage, but beware of them being too big, otherwise the birds will tend to slide to and fro during transport and this causes a lot of stress. Partitions should be included when transporting more than one bird.

Boxes made for the job have the advantage of being solid, but cardboard ones do not need periodic cleaning and take up no valuable storage space as they can be disposed of immediately after use. Make a cardboard box more secure by removing the flaps at the top and replacing them with a piece of hardboard cut fractionally oversize, and construct hinges and fasteners by threading wire or string through small holes pierced in the box and lid. Make sure your container has a solid base lined with a layer of newspapers, which can be covered with shavings or sawdust to absorb the droppings – although it must be said that hay or straw will allow the birds a better grip. No matter what sort of carry box is chosen, it goes without saying that it should be adequately ventilated and securely fastened.

Some waterfowl pens are only equipped with corrugated card, but it is far better if there is a good carpet of wood shavings that will absorb faeces and spilt water.

AT THE SHOW AND AFTER

Don't panic, and don't let yourself feel hassled. See the stewards and obtain your pen number. Take time in completing those last-minute preparations before settling the birds into their allocated pen, their home for the next few hours. If the pen hasn't sufficient floor covering, ask for a little more floor litter – some waterfowl pens are only equipped with corrugated card or paper, but it is far better if there's a good carpet of wood shavings that will absorb faeces: because the droppings of waterfowl are generally far looser than any other types of poultry, there is a very real possibility that watery droppings may adhere to the bird's plumage long before the judges reach your particular show pen.

Traditionally, birds were not fed or watered before judging, as a full crop could change the overall outline; however, it is probably kindest to provide a small water pot attached to the sides of the pen so that it cannot be spilt, and once judging has finished, it should be a prime objective to ensure that food and water are available. At

Small pens such as these are invaluable to the waterfowl enthusiast and have a multitude of uses – including the 'quarantining' of birds returning from shows and exhibitions.

117

many venues the stewards will undertake this task, but it is as well to check they have.

Normally you will not be allowed to remove your birds and take them home before a given time. Again, this could well be included in the rules and regulations found at the back of your schedule, but if not, ask a steward when you arrive in the morning.

After the Show

Care is as essential after the show as before. It is advisable to keep your returning birds as far away as possible from your other birds for at least a week after their return home, because if any disease has been contracted, it will be evident before they are returned to the flock. During the quarantine period, always care for your show birds after caring for your other birds, to reduce the possibility of transmitting disease.

EGG COMPETITIONS

Although most egg competitions are run by poultry show societies as a minor part of their overall event, it is also sometimes possible to find egg classes at village shows, and at those run by horticultural societies. A schedule is once again necessary to discover exactly what classes are available, and it will be no surprise to learn that even the humble egg has standards, and that a scale of points is looked for and awarded by experienced judges. Each egg will be given marks for its external uniformity and texture, and internally for freshness and colour. In the case of a plate of eggs being shown, each egg will be checked for its similarity in size, shape and colour to its neighbours on the plate.

Preparation for the Show

It is possible to wash eggs in preparation for showing, but it is better if the eggs can be kept clean naturally (not always an easy task when it comes to ducks and geese!) by using fresh straw in the nest boxes, and by changing any floor litter regularly so that dirt from the birds' feet is removed before they reach the nest boxes. Any odd specks of dirt on an otherwise clean egg can be gently removed with wire wool, though take care not to rub too hard and spoil the egg's natural bloom.

When a plate of eggs is being shown, each egg will be checked for its similarity in size, shape and colour to its neighbours on the plate.

Decorated Eggs

Although classes for decorated eggs are perhaps more often noticed at flower and craft shows than they are at some of the more serious poultry events, decorating and exhibiting duck and geese eggs can be an enjoyable pastime – especially as the size and texture of goose eggs in particular makes for a wonderful surface on which to work.

The idea of decorated eggs has been around for a long time, and several different design techiques have been developed. These include découpage, where patterned paper and glue is used; and sgraffito, a method by which layers of colour are painted on to the surface of an egg, and then patterns etched into them using a sharp-pointed instrument. Alternatively, if you have an artistic nature, you could try painting a countryside scene or even a portrait of the goose that laid the egg.

It is essential that the eggs are blown first of all: this is a relative-ly simple operation that involves piercing a small hole in the narrow end of an egg and a slightly larger one in the wider end; by insert-ing a cocktail stick in the bigger hole of the two, it should be possi-

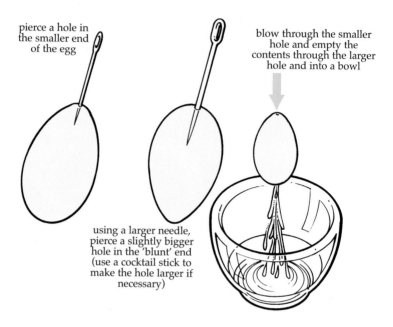

pierce a hole in the smaller end of the egg

blow through the smaller hole and empty the contents through the larger hole and into a bowl

using a larger needle, pierce a slightly bigger hole in the 'blunt' end (use a cocktail stick to make the hole larger if necessary)

Before decorating, it is essential that the eggs are blown first – a relatively simple operation that involves piercing a small hole in the narrow end of an egg and a slightly larger one in the wider end.

ble to enlarge it without cracking the egg. Hold the egg over a bowl, and blow hard through the small hole; it isn't easy, especially with a goose egg, but slowly and surely the yolk should come out. Once the egg is emptied of its contents, wash it through, perhaps with the aid of a syringe, then blow out the surplus water and place it somewhere warm so it can dry out.

SHOWING OPPORTUNITIES FOR YOUNG PEOPLE

Because so many people encouraged me when I was young, I am now a zealous advocate of encouraging youngsters into the poultry world. Most children have an affinity with ducks in particular – memories of Jemima Puddle-duck and Daffy Duck cartoons perhaps – and so, even if you are only half-heartedly reading this book with a view to possibly purchasing ducks and geese in the future, I urge you to buy at least a trio of Call ducks for your offspring.

Generally, it is not a good idea to suggest giving any sort of live-stock as a present unless you are absolutely sure that the intended recipient is knowledgeable enough and sufficiently enthusiastic to really want and appreciate the gift, but if children are correctly introduced to the hobby by a present of birds (complete with the necessary accessories), they will almost certainly become lifelong poultry enthusiasts.

Showing opportunities for youngsters sometimes arise as a result of their school having a rural studies area, or it has a 'fur and feather' club as an extra-curricular activity. Some schools are nowadays well known in the showing world, and in recent years birds that have been bred and cared for by their pupils have given experienced poultry fanciers a run for their money in several of the most prestigious shows.

Many small poultry clubs encourage junior members, and most show schedules include 'juvenile' classes; and judging by the show reports published in *Fancy Fowl* and *Feathered World*, there appears to be a ready supply of up-and-coming show enthusiasts, despite the media telling us that youngsters of the twenty-first century are becoming 'couch potatoes' and computer games' addicts. Long may this continue.

If children are correctly introduced to the show world and are fortunate enough to win prizes with their birds, they will almost certainly become lifelong poultry enthusiasts.

8

Ornamental Waterfowl

Whether this chapter should be called 'Ornamental Waterfowl' or 'Ornamental Wildfowl' is a moot point – personally, I consider 'waterfowl' to be more correct for the types of birds that may well have originated in the wild but are now commonly seen as part of a domesticated, 'non-utility' collection. Technically, however, as many of the bird types kept are strains of wildfowl – teal, for example – perhaps it should be 'Ornamental Wildfowl'! To add further to the confusion, The Pocket Oxford Dictionary describes waterfowl as being 'birds collecting in water', and wildfowl simply as 'game-birds'. As most people's collections will combine the two, I suppose the terminology matters little.

One thing that is certain is that the British Waterfowl Association looks after the interests of those who are enthusiastic keepers of both wildfowl and domestic waterfowl: there is, after all, an obvious and logical connection between the two with regard to habitat requirements and welfare. In addition, it is interesting to note that approximately two-thirds of their subscribers keep both types; no wonder, then, that much detailed specialist information is available on all types of waterfowl. Membership is therefore most strongly recommended.

TYPES TO CONSIDER

Many of the breeds of ducks and geese commonly found in private collections are of vulnerable status in the wild, and so one of your criteria might be choosing, keeping and rearing a particular type of waterfowl that will ensure its continuation. Specimens known for their colour variations could well be another. However, it is far more likely that your choice will be dictated by the costs involved in acquiring stock. A pair of young Red-breasted Geese (probably the most striking of all ornamental geese) could well set you back somewhere in the region of £225 per pair, whereas a pair of Ringed Teal,

---

Membership of the British Waterfowl Association

As a member, you will receive three magazines per annum, and there are, typically, two open days a year for BWA members to visit special collections. They also have a nationwide system of county representatives who can provide local contacts and advice, particularly with regard to ornamental waterfowl. The web site has down-loadable leaflets with articles about husbandry, and there is a bookshop providing some of the best publications on waterfowl.

---

for example, can be bought for as little as £30 and are therefore probably the cheapest of any of the smaller ducks to purchase.

The Ringed Teal, which originates from central South America, is also very popular with enthusiasts new to the hobby as it needs only a small aviary or pen containing a modest pond; furthermore they are very pretty and easily tamed. Unlike many other breeds of duck, both the male and female remain colourful throughout the year, which makes them well worth considering for their ornamental aspect – which is, after all, one of the main reasons for any addition

The Ringed Teal is popular with enthusiasts new to the hobby as they are very pretty and easily tamed.

to your flock. Pairs of Ringed Teal bond easily, and the females make good natural mothers.

Choosing a particular breed for their colour is, in most cases, quite straightforward and it is generally the male that displays a colourful plumage whilst the females can, at first glance, look quite drab. Look more closely however, and you may well find that the females have delicate markings, particularly around the head and eyes. Chiloe Widgeon and the Red-breasted Goose vary from the norm in that there is little difference between the sexes and both are particularly beautiful. Like the Chiloe Widgeon, Tufted Ducks nest on the ground and in thick vegetation close to the water's edge, but the Carolina Wood Duck, which along with the Mandarin is probably the most common duck type kept by ornamental waterfowl enthusiasts, much prefers to lay its eggs a few metres off the ground and in a hollow tree trunk or similar.

Given the chance, both Mandarins and Carolinas spend much of their time perched high up in the trees, and even in captivity love to perch on a branch positioned over the water. So not all wildfowl spend all their time on water: the Plumed Whistling Duck, for example, is not at all keen on swimming, and prefers instead to

The Red-breasted Goose varies from the norm in that there is little plumage difference between the sexes.

Although in this instance contentedly enjoying the water, Carolinas and Mandarins are equally at home perched in the trees.

spend its time in a group and on a bank where it can often be seen indulging in mutual preening. In appearance and stance it is, in fact, more like a goose than a duck.

The Ne-Ne, or Hawaiian Goose, is Hawaii's state bird, and during the mid-twentieth century became very scarce in its home of origin. Nowadays, however, it is seen in many waterfowl collections. It is, at first glance, very similar to the Canada Goose, with which we are all familiar, but unlike the Canada, which is the larger of the two, only the face, cap and hind-neck are black; also the Ne-Ne has buff-coloured cheeks. Unusually for any form of wildfowl, the Ne-Ne's feet are not completely webbed. Other geese suitable for consideration include the very sociable Barnacle, a very 'clean' and beautifully marked bird.

Some types of duck are surface feeders and others are divers. The Smew, for instance, dives deeply and swims under water, and as a result requires water of great depth. Many of the wildfowl known to shooting enthusiasts, including Pochard, will make very pretty and interesting additions to your flock providing the water is of sufficient depth, whilst others, such as the common Mallard, are surface feeders and require water only a matter of centimetres deep. (In

One of the types of geese suitable for consideration in a waterfowl collection of this nature is the sociable Barnacle, a very 'clean' and beautifully marked bird.

order to be able to submerge more easily, diving ducks are generally heavier size for size than surface-feeding ducks; a factor which causes them more difficulty in becoming airborne.)

HOUSING, FENCING AND PONDS

Generally, no specific housing is required, and if space is at a premium, the smaller species of duck will adapt well to netted aviaries: in fact they are best enjoyed in relatively small enclosures because otherwise they have a tendency to disappear into the distance of a large enclosure. Keeping ornamental ducks and geese outdoors without the protection of either a large pond on to which they can escape, or a fox-proof fenced enclosure (is there such a thing?), is foolhardy and expensive as you will be forever replacing your stock!

Fencing

To keep foxes out, it is probably a wise precaution to make the fence of two rolls of netting: a roll with 3.2cm (1¼in) mesh for the lower half, and one with 5cm (2in) mesh for the upper half. At least the bottom 30cm (1ft) should be turned out and buried under the turf, whilst the top 46cm (18in) is allowed to flop outwards. In this situation the overall height of the fencing must be at least 2m (6ft), so the height of the individual rolls of 3.2cm and 5cm mesh must reflect this, as well as the allocations needed to dig in and flop out.

Extra security is gained by adding an electric fence 23cm (9in) out from the base of the pen, and some 23cm above ground level, with a second strand being placed the same distance above the first. A third strand of electric wire could be attached to the top of the upright support posts – ensuring, of course, that it doesn't make contact with the floppy flange of wire mesh, in which case it will short out and be totally ineffective against predators.

Make sure that the gate is secured and that a piece of wire netting is buried directly below it so that nothing can dig and scratch its way underneath. It is also important to ensure that there are no corner posts set at an angle, because some of the more adventurous ducks could scramble up these and escape.

Ponds

Choosing the right spot for your pond may be as simple as selecting the only place available. Ideally you should try and locate an area where you can enjoy a view of your birds from as many points of the house and garden as possible, and where it will have five to six hours of sunshine every day. You may need to add tall grasses, shrubs or bushes to provide shade, but where practicable, try and incorporate whatever already exists.

Because a biological balance is easier to create and maintain in a larger pond than a smaller one, it is generally a good idea to make your pond as large as possible within the space allowed. However, the construction of a 'proper' landscaped pond is far beyond the scope of this book; note also that ponds of a certain size require permission from various local authorities.

Generally, a pond is likely to contain three different areas: a marshy zone around the perimeter, a shallow zone and a deep water area. Whether you choose a natural-looking pond lined with clay, or opt for the solution offered by flexible liners, you should be aware of the fact that simple round shapes are the least expensive, and excavation with creative curves and convoluted designs quickly adds to your start-up costs.

Inlet streams or a naturally occurring spring will help to circulate the water, and undoubtedly increases the health of the overall environment. It also increases the risk of predators entering the same

A pump or fountain through which water can be recycled from time to time will help in reoxygenating the water.

way, and so great care must be taken when fencing across any inlet and outlet sources. Similarly, you will need to allow for proper drainage during overflow caused by heavy rain, otherwise you may well find that a portion of your perimeter fencing has been washed away due to a build-up of flood debris against the wire.

Where such opportunities for constant fresh water do not exist, you may have to consider the installation of a pump through which water can be recycled from time to time. Remember, too, that duck excreta, stale food and decaying plant materials create ammonia, which is toxic, and if left unchecked, can be extremely harmful to your pond.

Plants Suitable for the Waterfowl Pond and Enclosure
The banks of any natural ponds can be planted up with shade-giving shrubbery; this will also help to keep the banks intact. Moreover, ducks and geese often nest closer together where brush or tall grass creates a visual barrier because this reduces territorial fighting. If possible, plant up any vegetation before introducing ducks and geese to the area; if not, protect it with wire netting, making sure

that this is tall enough so a bird cannot scrabble in and become trapped.

The following plants seem to be the most suitable in terms of indestructibility when planted in and around a waterfowl pen: ground ivy, silverweed, large-leafed butterbur, yellow iris, tall perennial grasses such as miscanthus and canary grass, and stinging nettles. In addition, low-growing conifers, Chinese juniper, dwarf spirea and soft fruit bushes such as gooseberry and raspberry will give some shade and protection from the wind and sun.

Plant check caused by the activities of waterfowl can be a problem, especially at the water's edge where marginal aquatics may be affected by the paddling of webbed feet, and damage to deep water aquatics with floating foliage can occur as a result of nibbling and 'grazing'. Some damage to floating foliage can be avoided by the simple expedient of growing those species and cultivars with the most robust leaves, whilst damage to marginal plants can be alleviated to some extent by establishing only those that will tolerate 15cm (6in) or more of water.

An artificially created pond containing an ideal mixture of water plants and bank-side vegetation. (Courtesy David Bland)

Islands

Islands have several advantages: as well as providing a relatively safe nesting site, they make good resting areas and feeding points, provide habitat for other wildlife, require little maintenance, and are long-lived if properly constructed. They will even provide habitat for other avian wildlife if they are large enough and contain sufficient natural vegetation – to this end, never stock your birds so densely that they decimate vegetation and bank sides. The only disadvantage to creating an artificial island is that initial costs can be high.

Islands are most easily built when the pond is being constructed or restored. Ideally, they should be situated about 20m (roughly 20yd) from the main shoreline in order to make predator access difficult, but that assumes a pond of a size that is not always an option to the small-scale enthusiast. Ideally, the top of the island should be 1m (1yd) higher than any anticipated high water level, with side slopes no steeper than 5:1 in exposed locations or 3:1 in sheltered spots or small ponds. The number of islands constructed depends upon the size of the pond and the size of the islands, but it is generally safe to assume one decent-sized island per half hectare (acre) of water.

Floating Islands

For cheapness, floating structures are probably your best option and have the advantages of being cheaper to construct, easy to maintain (they can be 'towed' back to shore for repairs, cleaning and checking nest boxes), and are not affected by water level fluctuations. They can also be easily installed in deep water. Their disadvantages are that they can become waterlogged and sink, and the nest boxes and the eggs they contain are easily accessible to rats.

Construct an artificial floating island by using telegraph poles or drums as floats, with rough wood spars attached both crossways and lengthways to make a frame. Small-mesh wire netting and some wads of straw (with the possible inclusion of a little topsoil) are all that are required to complete a platform, where suitable vegetation can then be planted. Such a construction will, of course, need to be anchored by weights, or by ropes attached to pegs on the bank side.

Nest Boxes for Waterfowl

In some breeds such as the Carolinas and Mandarins, the desire to be up amongst the tree branches is particularly strong when nesting

Construct an artificial floating island by using telegraph poles, rough wooden spars and small mesh wire netting. Floating islands need to be anchored by weights or ropes attached to pegs on the bank side.

– a legacy of their days in the wild when the females were entirely dependent on suitable nesting cavities in hollow tree trunks. This natural instinct can be accommodated by using raised nest boxes dotted around the enclosure, access to which can be gained from a nearby and strategically positioned branch. Other duck types vary in their requirements: the Ringed Teal, for example, only requires a small box with a small hole placed on the bank side or slightly tucked away in any available cover.

The best litter material to use in nest boxes is wood shavings, bark or good quality straw. A combination of large decorative bark and smaller chips or straw also works well. Each and every box should be inspected and refilled each year, preferably just before the birds begin to consider nesting in the early spring. You may well find that the wildfowl themselves make their own nests, filling them with sticks, leaves and grass, and if this material is dry and reasonably clean, there is no reason why it should not be left, although some new shavings could be added each year in order to ensure that the nest remains attractive to potential users.

Geese will generally prefer to lay and sit in nests open to the elements rather than in any specially constructed box (although

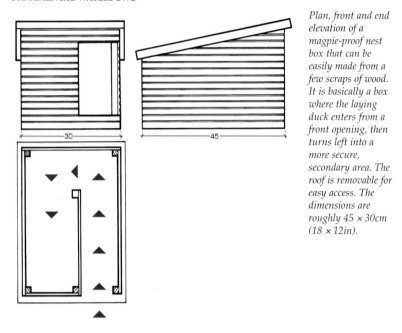

Plan, front and end elevation of a magpie-proof nest box that can be easily made from a few scraps of wood. It is basically a box where the laying duck enters from a front opening, then turns left into a more secure, secondary area. The roof is removable for easy access. The dimensions are roughly 45 × 30cm (18 × 12in).

Maned geese are very happy to use purpose-built raised boxes), and they will, if the vegetation is sufficient, make their own nest. If the start of a nest is noticed, you could assist by providing extra material in the form of straw or dried leaves saved from the previous autumn.

BREEDING AND REARING

Generally, ornamental waterfowl are bought, sold and kept as breeding pairs. Some types and strains bond with each other quite readily when placed together by the breeder, but others cannot be 'forced' into being together and much prefer to pick their own partners with which to mate. This bonding can be very strong in some breeds, and geese in particular will mourn the loss of a mate for quite some time in the unfortunate event of it dying naturally or being killed by predators. This mourning has been compared to clinical depression in humans and manifests itself as a dejected appearance: sunken, dull eyes and an unusually low head carriage.

Some breeds make better parents than others, and it is important to know the maternal capabilities of your chosen birds. You also need to be aware of the fact that females of different species may well choose to lay their eggs in the same nests in enclosures where several types are being kept together, which will obviously cause problems when it comes to one of the females going broody and commencing to sit – not the least of which being that different breeds may have different lengths of incubation. Where ornamental waterfowl are being kept as naturally as possible on a body of water, then their prospects for successfully raising a clutch of youngsters to maturity are poor – certainly when compared with their captive breeding in an aviary, or any other form of penned enclosure. Therefore as much as you might wish to keep things as nature intended, it is in fact probably easiest to collect eggs daily, and when you have sufficient, set them either under a broody chicken, or in an incubator.

To be sure of maintaining a pure-bred collection, one might consider penning particular breeding pairs in separated small aviaries so there can be no possibility of cross-mating between compatible breeds. Interestingly, despite being closely related, Mandarins and Carolinas cannot hybridize with each other due to the fact that the Mandarin has a different chromosomal composition to all other

Fertile eggs, suitably labelled and stored prior to incubation (note that their positioning by the window is for ease of the photography). Any eggs set aside for hatching purposes must always be kept in a cool, constant temperature.

ducks. Carolinas, on the other hand, can and will hybridize with many of the duck breeds.

FEEDING

When a balanced population of waterfowl is established, their life should, in theory at least, be self-sustaining. Practically however, the reality is somewhat different and subsistence has to be provided by means of regularly but sparingly distributed proprietary pellets and/or cereals. This should be fed twice a day at regular times allowing a small handful for each bird per feed. Hand feeding undoubtedly helps in maintaining a relationship between the birds and their owner so that when a problem arises they can be relatively easily captured and handled. Unfortunately, with the pressures and time restraints of day-to-day living, such attention to detail is not always possible, and there may be no alternative but to feed your ornamentals by means of ad lib hoppers. There are some very good ones available, some of which are designed with waterfowl in mind, but although they are weather-proof, unfortunately they are never vermin-proof, and you will find that, without a regular trapping programme or poison routine, they are a magnet to rats and wild birds.

No matter whether you are hand or hopper feeding, always move the feed site regularly in order to prevent any potential build-up of disease brought about by birds congregating and defecating in one area, and also to ensure that there is never any unnecessary wear and tear of the natural fabric of the water's edge.

Natural Food and Greenstuffs

All geese need a permanent supply of short grass for grazing, and provided that the area around the pond and certain areas of the enclosure produce a sufficient sward, they should only ever require a little additional feeding of breeder's pellets at the appropriate time, and perhaps the inclusion of some grain to their diet during the winter months. Live food such as earthworms will also be taken by many breeds of waterfowl, mealworms being a particular favourite. Some will also eat small frogs.

Pond weed is loved by all, and breeds such as the African White-backed Duck likes to feed on aquatic plants of all descriptions as well as any naturally occurring insects. African White-backs also much prefer millet to any other type of cereal that may be given as an additional diet, and so it might be worth considering the possibility of sowing a small, temporarily fenced area of the enclosure in order to grow some millet seed: once the crop is mature, the fence can be removed and the birds given access.

PREDATORS

You have, we hope, eliminated the possibility of your precious waterfowl collection falling victim to foxes, but there are several other potential predators that will need either controlling or eradicating entirely.

Rats are an ever-present problem whenever livestock of any kind is kept, and the environs of a waterfowl pond, with its ready supply of food and suitable sheltering places, provides an ideal habitat for them. They will, if left unchecked, make nests under nesting boxes, in the roots of shrubs, and around the base of any feed hoppers. Not only do rats eat vast quantities of food, they are also avid takers of eggs and newly hatched birds, as well as being known carriers of disease – some of which are harmful to humans. Their presence may

Poison baiting stations placed at regular intervals are the safest and most efficient means of eradicating rats.

at first go unnoticed, but once a colony has been established, their greasy-looking, smooth runs can be seen very easily. Provided that you keep the contents well away from your ducks and geese, poison baiting stations are the best option; they must, however, be kept continually checked and topped up, because if poison is given only spasmodically rats may build up an immunity by taking small quantities that are insufficient to be fatal.

Around the outside of the perimeter fence, it may pay to include a few tunnel traps: these are spring traps, such as the Fenn Mk IV, which can be bought from either gamekeeping or agricultural suppliers. The trap is covered by a 'tunnel' of three pieces of wood that protects any non-target species and helps to funnel the targeted predator through the openings at either end and towards the set trap positioned at the centre. Although you will most likely catch rats as they run around the base of the wire netting, tunnel traps are also very efficient at catching stoats and grey squirrels. Like rats, grey squirrels will take food and, on occasions, young birds. Stoats, despite being very attractive to look at, are very efficient and ruthless killers of both young and even adult ornamental ducks.

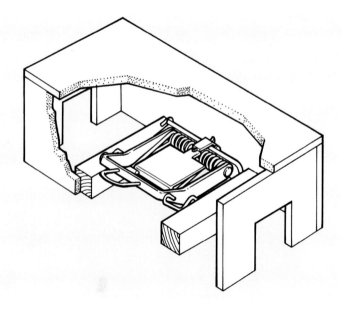

Spring traps such as the Fenn Mk IV are covered by a 'tunnel' of three pieces of wood, which protects any non-target species and helps to funnel the intended predators such as rats and stoats through the openings at each end.

Be aware of the fact that mink love the combination of water and a ready supply of food in the shape of your carefully nurtured birds. They will, given access and the opportunity, decimate waterfowl and are like foxes in that once the 'blood lust' affects them, will kill far more than they can ever hope to eat. Mink can climb well, but their most likely point of access will be where a natural stream runs through the pen, where it is more difficult to make the wire fence secure. Cage trapping is the usual means of catching them, but unless you intend purchasing a trap and keeping it permanently baited, you are perhaps best advised to contact Defra or a local gamekeeper should you ever be unfortunate enough to be visited by a wandering mink.

Avian predators such as crows and magpies love eggs and chicks and will enter seemingly safe and protected nest boxes in search of them. Larsen traps are the best way of keeping them in check. Larsen traps will catch at all times of the year, but their particular value is in catching crows and magpies when they set up their breeding territory – which, of course, coincides with the waterfowl breeding season. On the original design, the trap mechanism involves a spring door to each catching compartment, which, when set, is held open by a split perch. To enter the trap, birds have to drop on to the perch, which then gives way and the bird's momentum takes it past the bottom of the door, which flips up. The only slight disadvantage to the system is that to work well, it needs a live decoy – which is not always easy to acquire, although a local game-keeper can sometimes help in this respect.

Last, but certainly not least, never forget that cats, especially feral ones, are surprisingly efficient predators and can climb the posts of most enclosures with very little difficulty.

MOULTING

The eclipse plumage in ducks was described by Charles Darwin as being 'a plumage of inconspicuous hues designed to aid the drakes in concealing themselves during that period when they have moulted all their wing feathers and are unable to fly'. Others, however, have regarded it simply as being winter or non-breeding plumage as distinct from summer or 'nuptial' plumage.

In domestic waterfowl (and indeed any other form of domestic poultry), birds will moult and lose their feathers annually, at some time during late summer and early autumn. Ornamental waterfowl are different in that they will sometimes have what is known as a 'double moult', where the males will go into 'eclipse' immediately after the breeding period and will then moult back into breeding plumage in the autumn.

Many species of duck are temporarily flightless while moulting, and in the wild, moulting would, typically, precede migration. The length of period the eclipse lasts also varies, and it has been noticed that the male Mallard, for example, will lose his definitive plumage for perhaps as long as three months, whereas the Pintail male is only in eclipse for two months. Interestingly and inexplicably, some breeds remain colourful throughout the year, as for example the Ringed Teal.

The primary purpose of moulting is to replace old, worn-out feathers with new ones. The feather-growing process requires a great deal of energy, and most moults begin with the loss of the innermost primary feathers on both wings. When about half the primaries are affected, it continues to the outermost secondary feathers on the wings. The bird then begins to moult body feathers, lastly followed by the tail. During this period, it might, where possible, be beneficial to feed food known to contain a slightly higher protein level than normal, as this will help in promoting the best possible feather formation.

The males of most species acquire their breeding plumage in the autumn.

Useful Addresses

MAGAZINES

Country Smallholding
Archant Devon, Fair Oak Close, Exeter Airport Business Park,
Clyst Honiton, Near Exeter, EX5 2UL
Tel: 01392 888481
Email: editorial.csh@archant.co.uk

Fancy Fowl
The Publishing House, Station Road, Framlingham,
Suffolk, IP13 9EE
Tel: 01728 622030
Email: fancyfowl@todaymagazines.co.uk
Web: www.fancyfowl.com

Smallholder
Hook House, Hook Road, Wimblington, March,
Cambridgeshire, PE15 0QL
Tel: 01354 741583
Email: liz.wright1@btconnect.com
Web: www.smallholder.co.uk

ASSOCIATIONS AND ORGANIZATIONS

British Waterfowl Association
Sue Schubert, PO Box 163, Oxted, Surrey, RH8 0WP
Tel: 01892 740212
Email: info@waterfowl.org.uk
Web: www.waterfowl.org.uk

Call Duck Association
Graham Barnard, Ty Cwmdar, Cwrt-y-Cadno,
Llanwrda, Carmarthenshire, SA19 8YH
Tel: 01558 650532
Email: callducks@online.co.uk
Web: www.callducks.net

Domestic Waterfowl Club of Great Britain
Mike Hatcher, Limetree Cottage, Brightwalton,
Newbury, Berkshire, RG20 7BZ
Tel: 01488 638014

Indian Runner Duck Association
Christine Ashton, Red House, Hope,
Welshpool, SY21 8JD
Tel: 01938 554011
Email: runnerdux@yahoo.co.uk
Web: www.runnerduck.net

Glossary

Addled A fertile egg, the embryo of which has died during incubation.

Air sac Air space found at the broad end of the egg.

Ark Small portable house for ducks or geese.

Axial feather Short wing feather found between the primary and secondary flight feathers.

Bean Dark, horny, triangular patch on the top of the beak on some ducks.

Blood spot Spot seen in the laid egg; the reasons for its appearance could be due to generic and/or nutritional causes.

Brood spot Bare patch found on the breast of a broody female.

Candling Using a strong source of light to reveal the contents of the whole egg and judge its fertility.

Caruncles Fleshy protruberances on the head and neck of the Muscovy duck and drake.

'Clears' Infertile eggs found after candling.

Coop Small shelter, usually used to house sitting hens and/or chicks.

Crop Place in which food is stored after swallowing, but before it travels through to the stomach and gizzard.

Dewlap Visible part of the throat or gullet often seen in breeds of geese.

Drake Male duck.

Duck General term, but more accurately used to denote the female of the species.

Eclipse Term used to describe the early summer moult of ornamental drakes.

Egg tooth Small 'spike' at the tip of the upper beak; it enables the duckling to chip its way out of the egg and disappears several hours after hatching.

Electric energizer Unit used to supply power to electric fencing.

Flight feathers The large primary feathers in the last half of the wing.

Fold unit Movable combined house and run.

Gander Male goose.

Gizzard Grinding stomach with muscular lining for pulping food.

Goose General term, but more accurately used to denote the female of the species.

Hybrid The result of crossing two or more strains, breeds or families within a breed. It will not breed true and reproduce chicks in its own likeness.

Infra-red Type of heating used for rearing chicks.

Keel Bony ridge of the breast-bone. Also, skin found hanging down from it in some ducks and geese.

Keyes trays Flat fibre trays used for egg storing.

Mandible Lower or upper half of beak.

Moulting The period when a bird sheds its old feathers and re-grows new ones; generally occurs in the late summer/early autumn.

Parson's nose *See* 'Preen gland'.

Pinioning Involves the permanent removal of the manus, or outer part of the wing, and is usually done in the early stages of a duckling/gosling's life.

Preen gland Oil-producing gland at the base of the rump (also known as the parson's nose).

Roach back Deformity of the vertebrae showing as a hunched back.

Secondary feathers Quill feathers on the wing, which are usually visible when the wings are either folded or extended.

Split wing A deformity of the wing that shows itself when the axial feather is missing. It is thought to be hereditary and it is therefore best not to breed from any bird displaying this fault.

Stubbing After plucking, the removal of new developing feathers.

Trachea Otherwise known as the windpipe and part of the respiratory system, which allows air to pass from the larynx to the lungs and bronchi. Sometimes the trachea can be affected by dust and worm infections.

Treading Action of the male bird mating with the female.

Vent Rear 'opening' through which droppings and eggs are excreted.

Wet plucking Traditionally preferred method of plucking downy-feathered birds such as ducks and geese.

Wing clipping Sometimes it is necessary to clip the primary and secondary feathers of one wing to prevent lighter breeds such as ornamental or Call ducks from flying. The feathers will regrow in the next moult.

Index